FIGHTING BACK

What the Bible Says About Spiritual Warfare

GIL STIEGLITZ

Fighting Back: What the Bible Says About Spiritual Warfare
© 2026 Gil Stieglitz. All rights reserved.

Published by PTLB Publishing, P. O. Box 214, Roseville, CA 95661, PTLB.com.

Copyedited and produced by Jennifer Edwards, jedwardsediting.net

Cover and interior design by Ben Holman

Cover Photo Credit: Pixabay

Author photo credit: Hannah White

Interior photo credits: Ron Lach (opposite pgs 1, 12, 16, 40, 56, 72, 84, 104, 110, 113, 120, and 132), RDNE Stock Project (pg 16), Mikhail Nilov pg 16), Ketut Subiyanto (pg 63), Nay Nyo (pg 63), Pavel Danilyuk (pg 63), Yugi Gdu (pg 70), Yan Krukau (pg 70), Deepak Maurya (pg 70), Two Shores (pg 98), Andrea Placquadio (pg 98), Pixabay (pg 101), Arina Krasnikova(pg 113), Oladimeji Ajegbile (pg 113), Gustvo Fotografo (pg 113).

Noncommercial interests may reproduce portions of this book without the express written permission of the author, provided the text does not exceed five hundred words. When reproducing text from this book, include the following credit line: "*Fighting Back* by Dr. Gil Stieglitz. Used by permission."

Commercial interests: No part of this publication may be reproduced, stored in a retrieval system, or transmitted in any way by any means: electronic, mechanical, photocopy, recording, or otherwise, without the prior permission of the copyright holder, except as provided by USA copyright law.

All Scripture verses are taken from the *New American Standard Bible* unless otherwise indicated. New American Standard Bible: 1995 update. La Habra, CA: The Lockman Foundation.

ISBN: 978-1-952736-06-3 (paperback)
  978-1-952736-07-0 (e-book)
  978-1-952736-08-7 (audiobook)

Library of Congress Catalog Number: 2025926444
PRINTED IN THE UNITED STATES OF AMERICA

DEDICATION

This book is dedicated to the men and women of the Bayside Action Groups.

I am so encouraged by how you are growing and fighting back against the World, the Flesh, and the Devil. God is using you to make a difference in the world, and it will only grow. It is such a privilege to help you dive deep into the wonder of God and see Him reveal Himself to you individually.

CONTENTS

Introduction i

Round 1: The Goal of Spiritual Warfare. 1

Round 2: The Three Levels of Spiritual Warfare 13

Round 3: The Three Stages of Christian Growth 41

Round 4: Understanding Enemy #1: The World 57

Round 5: Weapon #1: Do Not Love the World. 73

Round 6: Understanding Enemy #2: The Flesh. 85

Round 7: Weapon #2: Die to the Flesh. 95

Round 8: Understanding Enemy #3: The Devil. 105

Round 9: Weapon # 3: Resist the Devil 111

Round 10: Weapon #4: Put on the Armor of God 121

Conclusion 145

Notes 151

About the Author. 153

Other Resources by PTLB. 154

INTRODUCTION

Approximately two years ago, a delightful young couple, whom we will call Paul and Connie, approached me about discipling them at a deeper level so they could grow closer to God and learn to help others in spiritual warfare. The young man, Paul, is sharp, aggressive, and eager to battle the Devil, but I had to let him know that he would need to learn how to love God at a new level before he'd be ready to take on great battles in spiritual warfare. Connie is calm, godly, and deeply in love with the Lord. Together, they have been growing by leaps and bounds in their love for the Lord and their service for Him.

The most exciting thing about their growth in Christ is their realization that the greatest part of their spiritual war is in raising their five children. Paul has renewed his efforts to be a better father and a better man, and Christ is rewarding him with many wins. I am very impressed by how both Paul and Connie are loving the Lord and their family. Spiritual war is not usually about battling demons directly; it is often about cooperating with God to love the most important people in your life. Paul seems designed and gifted by God to help others in spiritual warfare in the future, and it is exciting to see his growth. God will use Paul and Connie to help many in their spiritual battles because they are doing so well at loving the Lord, their children, and their friends.

What I see in Paul and Connie was reproduced over and over again in the early church. Individual Christians and the Christian church as a whole were a dynamic force in the first four hundred years of Christianity. Despite hostile spiritual, religious, and governmental forces raised up against it, the Christian church changed the world. People flocked to Christianity so they could have a personal relationship with the One True God, and because it was the only place where they could be permanently liberated from the spirits, temptations, and wickedness of the ancient world.

The early church was dynamic because it trained Christians to know God and His character, understand the Enemy's tactics, and how to use all the weapons of righteousness that the Lord Jesus Christ provided them (2 Corinthians 6:7). Equipped with dozens of spiritual weapons from God, average Christians were able to create a life of freedom, dignity, love, and joy, which was virtually unknown in the ancient world. Using the weapons of righteousness allowed them to build a spiritual force field around their lives, shielding them from the wickedness around them. They were in the world, but they were not of it. They knew they were in a spiritual war, and they were ready for it. They not only survived but thrived in the midst of exactly the kind of wickedness that infects our society today.

It was through the training provided by those churches in the first three hundred years—not through a school, university, or graduate course—that Christians began to live a different kind of life. With practice, they learned how to identify the Enemy, understand which weapon to use for a specific attack, and deploy the weapons effectively. They became skilled and fully equipped for any spiritual battle they faced.

Unfortunately, the modern church is only now beginning to acknowledge the spiritual nature of the war with sin. Most churches today still don't acknowledge the need for spiritual battle training, let alone provide consistent training systems to fully equip Christians. It's almost as if we're fighting the Enemy with one hand tied behind our backs; it doesn't have to be that way any longer.

This book aims to reintroduce the Christian church to the enemies and weapons that Jesus and the apostles describe in the New Testament. As Christians become thoroughly equipped with these weapons of righteousness, they will learn how to fight the Enemy effectively and become completely free. Once that happens, the church will become dynamic once again. With great anticipation and hope, I watch as numerous individuals, churches, and organizations begin to speak into the spiritual war we all face, but we need a more systematic and practical form of training. I hope this guide will offer a template for unleashing the power of Christ in Christians and in His Bride, the Church.

It is essential to understand that everyone lives in the midst of a spiritual battle. Spiritual warfare is all around us. Since many people are confused about what spiritual warfare actually is, let me define it for you. Spiritual warfare is our struggle to love God, others, and ourselves righteously. The World, the Flesh, and the Devil make it hard for us to fulfill Jesus's commands to love God with all our heart, soul, mind, and strength, and our neighbors as ourselves (Matthew 22:37–39). At times, spiritual warfare may involve cases of demons inhabiting a person's body, but this is in extreme cases. The primary arenas of spiritual war are our thoughts, choices, emotions, and actions. God is in us to will and to work His good pleasure, but our enemies do all they can to keep us from being loving and righteous people (Philippians 2:12–14).

Spiritual warfare is the struggle to love others who don't deserve it in a broken, sinful world (Ephesians 6:13). The attacks of spiritual warfare consist of the thoughts to do evil that fly through our minds, or choices that suggest themselves to us, tempting us to act on them even though we know they are wrong. It is the emotions of fear, despair, anger, depression, and hatred that seek to overwhelm us, keeping us from doing God's ideal for us. Each one of these things can be likened to bullets, arrows, and explosives used in real war.

In our regular lives, there are people to love, a mighty God to worship and glorify, and our God-given purposes to honor and accomplish. A medical doctor's job is to help people be healthy so they can live their lives, while physical diseases and injuries come uninvited to damage and destroy our ability to live normally. Likewise, our Christian lives are attacked by spiritual enemies, spiritual diseases, and spiritual injuries that can cause us to not be loving, to not be righteous, and to not fulfill our purpose.

Fortunately, God has given us a vast arsenal of spiritual weapons to protect us and push back the spiritual darkness that seeks to keep us from being loving and righteous people. Some of these weapons protect us from the spiritual diseases that come from sin, and some create new levels of spiritual calm in our lives by directing us to wholesome and righteous activities.

I would doubt anyone would disagree that evil is growing and abounding in our country and world today. Injustice, abuse, and oppression are everywhere. So, if we know from Scripture that the number one goal of life for a Christian is to love God, love others, and love oneself righteously, and the Devil's number one goal is to prevent real love from happening or pervert it into something destructive, then we have a real battle on our hands. Join me in learning how to love the people you are supposed to love, glorify and worship God with gusto, and fulfill your individual God-given purpose.

Over the past forty-plus years, the Church as a whole has been producing incredibly weak Christians. This book aims to change that. We need Christians who know how to live out their faith with weapons at the ready. If injustice is to be corrected, we need fully developed Christians who understand and are skilled with God's weapons of righteousness.

How do we become stronger so we can make a difference? The apostle Paul faced a world full of every kind of injustice and oppression, just like we do today (political, religious, occupational, mental, emotional). Tucked away in a little verse written to the Corinthians is God's answer to our question. Second Corinthians 6:7 says, "in the word of truth, in the power of God; by the weapons of righteousness for the right hand and the left ..." God's answer is to become aware of our enemies and become proficient at using the weapons of righteousness.

How can you sense an enemy's attack? How do you know if it's the World, the Flesh, or the Devil attacking you? Which of these Christian enemies is giving you the most trouble right now? I want you to realize that the

INTRODUCTION

World seeks to change your thinking until God's things don't seem desirable or seem too limiting. The Flesh seeks to have you give in to the selfishness inside of you. The Devil and his minions seek to overwhelm you with emotions, stray thoughts, or evil choices so that you will miss God's best because you are distracted, oppressed, or addicted to a particular pleasure, or actively choosing to embrace the overwhelming emotion. Come and learn how to resist these enemies' attacks, temptations, and oppressions. God's Word has told us how to win and what winning looks like. Now all we need to do is learn and obey.

For years, I have been helping people grapple with all levels of spiritual warfare, from simple temptation to severe demonic oppression. In every case, the weapons that Christ has given us are adequate when we use them. As I have helped hundreds of people deepen their faith, prepare for ministry, and/or escape the clutches of the Devil, it is knowing who the enemy is and how to use the weapons of righteousness that have carried the day. I offer this guide as an opportunity to train for and win during times of spiritual warfare. May God bless our efforts.

ROUND 1

The Goal of Spiritual Warfare

As a pastor, I often work with people who have some level of chaos going on in their lives. I remember working with a young woman who became aware of the depth of how the Devil had been influencing, attacking, and even oppressing her personally. We prayed together, and soon she confessed, repented, and renounced all known sin in her life. She was free.

Or so we thought. Sadly, she was so incensed by the level of influence that the Devil was able to have in her life and in her family's life that she began to attack her mother and her family for allowing sins and curses to be pronounced over her and the whole family. She became anything but loving toward her mother and family. She thought she was railing against the Devil, but she ended up railing against her actual family members. She needed to cancel out any curses and sins of the past, but she became lost for over two years in her search for sins and the Devil instead of ways to love her family in the Lord's power.

The overall goal of spiritual warfare is loving God, loving others, and loving yourself righteously (Matthew 22:37–39). This is what Jesus said when He was asked what the greatest command in Scripture is. We need to realize that God primarily wants to empower us, direct us, and bless us so that we can be great lovers in this world and the next. Success is not about money, power, fame, sex, pleasure, or any of the other things that our world clamors for … it is about becoming a great lover of God, others, and ourselves righteously. Let's take a look at a few verses from the Bible that will help our spiritual compass point back to true north.

> One of them, a lawyer, asked Him a question, testing Him, "Teacher, which is the great commandment in the Law?" And He said to him, 'YOU SHALL LOVE THE LORD YOUR GOD WITH ALL YOUR HEART, AND WITH ALL YOUR SOUL, AND WITH ALL YOUR MIND.' This is the great and foremost

commandment. The second is like it, 'You ou shall love your neighbor as yourself.' On these two commandments depend the whole Law and the Prophets." (Matthew 22:35–41)

"Little children, I am with you a little while longer. You will seek Me; and as I said to the Jews, now I also say to you, 'Where I am going, you cannot come.' A new commandment I give to you, that you love one another, even as I have loved you, that you also love one another. By this all men will know that you are My disciples, if you have love for one another." (John 13:33–35)

But the goal of our instruction is love from a pure heart and a good conscience and a sincere faith. (1 Timothy 1:5)

For this reason I bow my knees before the Father, from whom every family in heaven and on earth derives its name, that He would grant you, according to the riches of His glory, to be strengthened with power through His Spirit in the inner man, so that Christ may dwell in your hearts through faith; and that you, being rooted and grounded in love, may be able to comprehend with all the saints what is the breadth and length and height and depth, and to know the love of Christ which surpasses knowledge, that you may be filled up to all the fullness of God. (Ephesians 3:14–19)

For our struggle is not against flesh and blood … (Ephesians 6:12)

These verses teach us that if we become preoccupied with the Devil, he wins because we are not doing the thing God says is most important—loving God, the people in our lives, or ourselves in a righteous way. If we are constantly monitoring how we are being tempted by our flesh to be selfish, we miss opportunities to be loving because we are self-focused on fleshly sins. If we are overwhelmed by a particular culture's immoral suggestions and encouragements, we may miss chances to love God, the people around us, and even ourselves rightly. Everything the World does aims to prevent us from becoming better lovers. Everything the Devil does distracts, influences, and traps us so we cannot love God and the people we're meant to love, let alone ourselves, in a righteous way. All that our fleshly, selfish, and sinful nature seeks is to keep us focused on unholy desires, so we don't notice the love God is giving us.

I worked with a young woman from South Africa years ago who was so angered by how her family had earned their wealth and participated in the cruel racial segregation in their country that she started to hate her family and disavow even the good and righteous things they had done for her. Yes, she needed to confess their sins as wrong and the sins that she had committed. Yes, she needed to stand up for everyone's rights, but she also needed to grow in her ability to love her family members despite knowing the truth. She became estranged for several years because she was so focused on fighting the World System and the corruption it always brings. She wasn't loving others well.

I remember another woman who came to faith in Christ from a bizarre cult where false angels appeared to her. When she heard the truth of the gospel, she was immediately broken by the sacrifice of Christ and her arrogance and selfishness. She began to grow and became aware of the sins of the Flesh that constantly pushed their way into her life. This led her to focus on overcoming these sins. She became so focused on the fleshly sins that seemed to stir constantly within her that she began to fast regularly from food and to enter into prolonged times of prayer during the night watches. She basically denied herself even the basic comforts of warmth, food, and shelter in order to die to the flesh.

One time, she came to me and asked if I thought she should fast for three weeks to become a better Christian. Concerned, I told her that if she fasted in her fragile state for three weeks, she might very well see Jesus face-to-face in heaven. Instead of focusing on the one true goal of being a Christian—loving God, loving others, and loving herself righteously—her focus was on the sins of the Flesh, which had become unhealthy. She was not loving herself righteously, which meant she lacked the energy to love others. She needed adequate sleep, proper nutrition, and the presence of friends, fun, and joy, rather than constantly fixating on her fleshly sins in mind, body, and emotions. Our church elders prayed with her and realized that the whole church needed to fast one day each week for the next three weeks to prepare for the spiritual season ahead. It was a victory for the entire church and for her. She needed to be able to receive love and give it from a healthy personal space.

The most successful people in life are those who are growing in these three areas of love: God, others, and self (righteously). This is the goal of all spiritual warfare. If the World, the Flesh, or the Devil has you focused on something else other than what God commands, you're losing the spiritual war. I've prepared the following exercises to help you know what loving God, others, and yourself looks like. Just like with anything worthwhile, it requires practice.

SPIRITUAL EXERCISES
Loving God, Others, and Self Righteously

1. How will you love God in the next seven days? I've developed several spiritual exercises to help you express love to God. Some of these are meant to be done every day, while others can be done weekly or as the Lord leads.

    - I will confess my sins to the Lord every night at the end of the night, using the Seven Deadly Sins as my prayer sheet: Pride, Envy, Anger, Lust, Sloth, Gluttony, and Greed.

    - I will listen to the promptings of the Holy Spirit to love, be joyful, promote peace, be patient, express kindness, do something good for someone, control my emotions, stay faithful, and be self-controlled (Fruit of the Spirit).

    - I will repeat a section of Scripture throughout the day that God has directed me to:

        From the Proverb of the day ...

        From the Lord's prayer ...

        From the 23rd Psalm ...

        From the book of Philippians ...

        From the book of James ...

From the Beatitudes …

From the Great Commandments and/or the Ten Commandments …

- I will study a particular Bible passage that God has directed me toward as His message for me today.

- I will ask God for what I need for the day and for others' needs.

- I will praise God for a number of the good things in my life.

- I will adore God for who He is: All-wise, All-knowing, All-powerful, Sovereign, Holy, True, Faithful, Everywhere present, Good, Loving, Righteous.

- I will go to a church service this week and a midweek meeting to grow and connect with other believers.

- I will identify with Christ through baptism, communion, or being ready to witness to what He has done for my life.

- I will be open to God prompting me to abstain from food, talking, sleep, or friends for a set amount of time to be more focused on Him.

- I will ask Him to use me to meet the needs of the people around me in some specific way—

listening, helping, explaining, giving funds, or serving in some way.

2. How will you love the people in your life in the next seven days? Loving someone means meeting a need they have, pursuing them through listening, and/or pleasing them in a specific way that is meaningful to them.

- Ask God how you would have to adjust your current schedule to love your spouse, your children, your co-workers, your neighbors, and your friends this next week. It doesn't have to be a big thing; in fact, it is best to start small and listen to the Lord's prompting to do a small thing rather than some huge thing.

3. How are you going to love yourself righteously this next week? This usually means looking at healthy amounts of:

- Sleep
- Nutrition
- Exercise
- People time
- Alone time
- Personal Hygiene

PRAYER
Show Me How to Love

Dear Heavenly Father,

I come in the Name of the Lord Jesus Christ, asking you to show me how to love You with all my heart, soul, mind, and strength. Show me how to schedule time for the spiritual exercises to hear from You. I ask for Your power and Your wisdom to add YOU to my schedule more. I also ask You to show me what to remove from my schedule so I can do this.

Lord, I also ask You to prompt me to love all the crucial people in my life at the right time and in the right ways, both small and big. I will listen. I assume that there is more love that I can show to the people in my life and that many times I am just too self-focused. Guide me, Lord, and empower me when I don't feel the energy or a natural willingness to act in righteous, loving ways toward these important people. Lord, I know I will not be perfect, but I really do want to grow in this area.

Lord, I also need to grow in righteously loving myself. I do not need to love my selfish tendencies, but I do need to love the spiritual me, the mental me, the emotional me, the physical me, and the relational me in healthy, righteous ways. Direct me,

Lord, in ways to strengthen myself in all of the above areas so I can be Your agent wherever You send me. I thank You that You know me more than I know myself. You know the areas where I am not paying enough attention to what I really need. Please prompt me to get more rest, eat better, commune with You, exercise more (or less), and spend time with different people if that is what I really need. Lord, I know that You want me to be healthy and energetic even more than I do ... so please guide and empower me in this area also.

Lord, thank You for making the goal of spiritual warfare not defeating the Devil but loving You, others, and myself. Thank You for giving me the tools to do these things in Your Word and in the Holy Spirit. Show me how to accomplish this clear goal in my present circumstances and with my present knowledge and skills. I know I will keep growing in these areas throughout my life. Don't let me get so caught up with the Devil or even Your power over Him that I miss growing in love, which is the real goal.

In the Name of the Lord Jesus Christ,

Amen

ROUND 2

The Three Levels of Spiritual Warfare

Many of us who have become involved in demonic deliverance have noticed three levels in the Devil's work against people. These are often described as mild, moderate, and severe. We can see these levels of bondage to the Devil and sin in the Scriptures.

Examples of mild persecution are when Jesus faces temptation from the Devil in Matthew 4 and when the Devil tries to use Peter to distract Jesus from fulfilling His mission of salvation in Matthew 16.

Moderate persecution occurred when Jesus was preaching in the various synagogues in Galilee, and He cast out the demons afflicting the people in the various services, as told in Mark 1:39.

Severe persecution occurred when the father brought the boy, who was fully demonized and threw himself into the flames at times, in Matthew 17, and when the Gadarene demoniacs, who could not be bound and were living among the tombs, were delivered by Jesus in Matthew 8:28.

As my team and I seek to help people, it is helpful to know that these levels of temptation, sin, and bondage exist. The person who wants to be free needs to confess their sins, turn away from what they have done, and renounce whatever is giving the demons the right to plague their life. All of us have sinned and fallen short of the glory of God (Romans 3:23), so we must surrender to Jesus Christ for the forgiveness of our sins as our Savior and our Lord (Romans 10:9–10). But when we come to Christ, He wants to begin the sanctifying process where He sets us apart from our sins (Philippians 2:12–14) and to make us holy as He is holy (1 Peter 1:16). The process of sanctification will not be complete until we see Him in Heaven (1 John 1:1–3).

The consequence of sin is that it holds us back from loving God, loving others, and loving ourselves righteously. I talk with people all the time about the possible influence of the Devil in their lives, and yet they do not realize that it is because of sin in almost every case that he is able to tempt, attack, influence, and even oppress them (Job was an exception). We have become blind to the destructive power of sin in our lives.

A number of years ago, I saw a scriptural connection between the types of sins committed and the level of demonic bondage. There are three types of sin clearly mentioned in the Bible: Sins of Omission,[1] Sins of Commission,[2] and Sins of Wickedness.[3] The three levels of demonic attack and influence seem directly tied to these types of sins. Sins of Omission are tied to mild or normal levels of spiritual attack. Sins of Commission are tied to moderate or stronger forms of temptation and spiritual oppression. Sins of Wickedness are tied to the most severe and oppressive, even possessive forms of demonic attack.

The Christian Life: Learning to Love God, Others, Self within the 10 Commandments (Matt. 22:37-39; 1 Tim. 1:5).

Three Levels of Spiritual Warfare

There are 3 zones of spiritual warfare due to 3 kinds of sins in the Bible.

SINS OF OMISSION

Notice in the diagram above how these three levels work in the everyday life of the believer. Believers are meant to live a life of love within the boundaries of the Ten Commandments. This is the normal Christian life. We can be tempted and even attacked in Zone 1 to commit Sins of Omission, actions we choose not to do that we ought to do in regard to each major relationship in our lives.

God tells us how to live a righteous and loving life in the Scriptures. When I use the word "love," I am not talking about feeling an overwhelming desire for the other person. To love biblically means to meet needs, pursue, and please. Love is doing for the other person that they need.

God wants us to cooperate with Him on building a great and blessed life in each of our major relationships. We have to realize that there are instructions and commands in the Scriptures for each of these areas of life. If we cooperate with Him and begin doing what He suggests and commands, our life in that area usually goes better (unless the other person is so selfish and sinful that they do not respond to you meeting their needs, pursuing them, or pleasing them). If we don't cooperate, things aren't as good as they could be due to sin. Let me give you a few examples of Sins of Omission from what I call the nine relational gardens, which are outlined in the diagram below.

We all have 9 major relationships. God wants to maximize these. (Matt 22:37; John 10:10)

Marriage	Family	Work
Finance	GOD	Friends
Church	Society	Self

Pray for each of these areas.   PTLB.com

In the relational garden of marriage, God tells husbands to love their wives as Christ loved the church. If a husband fails to do that, he is committing a Sin of Omission and thus misses out on the blessings of a great marriage. In a sense, he is sinning against himself as well as God. He should confess his sin to God and ask for guidance on how he can love his wife in this sacrificial way. There are seven major actions that God tells husbands to do to build a great marriage, and I highly recommend you investigate them.[4]

Likewise, God has given at least seven different commands that a wife should do to bless her marriage and love her husband.[5] One example of a command is found in Ephesians 5:22, where Christ tells wives to adapt to their husbands. If she does adapt to her husband, then the marriage significantly improves, and she receives the blessing. If she does not adapt, then she is committing a Sin of Omission.

In the garden of parenting, God instructs children to honor their father and their mother (Ephesians 6:1–3). If they fail to do that, it is a Sin of Omission. Failing to honor their father and mother results in them missing out on the blessing of a healthy family, which will be a less loving and enjoyable place to be due to their sin. Yes, I know that many parents do dishonorable things, and yet there are often ways to fulfill this command by focusing on the parent's good points. God tells parents, and especially fathers, not to exasperate their children but to bring them up in the nurture and admonition of the Lord (Ephesians 6:4). If parents fail to do this, then they have failed to love their children and have committed Sins of Omission.

In the garden of vocation, career, and work, God tells us in various places in Scripture to be a hard worker and earn a living (Ephesians 6:5–8; Colossians 3:22–25). If we are lazy and too dependent on others, then we are committing Sins of Omission (Proverbs 6:6–11). If we fail to be hard-working and diligent, we are committing Sins of Omission (Proverbs 10:4; 13:4). God gives us instructions on how to treat employees if we are business owners or managers (Ephesians 6:9). He tells us how to be a Christian employee that glorifies God (Ephesians 6:5–8).

In the finance and money garden, He gives numerous commands about how you earn your income, how you manage your money, and how generous you need to be (Proverbs 27:23–27; Proverbs 15:27; Malachi 3:10; Matthew 23:23). Whole companies have been built around teaching proven biblical money principles, which have helped thousands of people.[6] In the personal garden, there is the clear command to be positive with our words and not destructive, sarcastic, or negative

(Ephesians 4:29). And yet many Christians see this as a suggestion and do not realize that they are committing Sins of Omission when they miss the chance to build people up or encourage others with a positive word. In every area of life, God has given us instructions on how to live and create a righteous, loving life. If we fail to do those things, then we are committing Sins of Omission.

The modern church has largely stopped teaching that the commands of Scripture come with consequences for disobedience and blessings for obedience. This may be due to legalism and arrogance, which can subtly influence a church that already emphasizes the Sins of Omission. But the Old and New Testaments are full of clear guidance on how to live a life of blessing and love. It is this life of love that our spiritual enemies are most interested in stopping. They want to distract us, damage us, anger us, and destroy us so that we cannot be the lovers of God, lovers of others, and righteous lovers of ourselves that we should be.

I am deeply concerned that Christians today are told to fight against Trespass Sins and Wicked Sins, but we are missing the Sins of Omission. It is in the positive commands of Scripture that the Christian life of joy, love, peace, and wonder is built. Do not allow spiritual warfare to keep us from the love we should show to God and those around us.

If we followed God's instructions and commands on what to positively do, our relationships would change. God wants to guide us with His Holy Spirit and instruct us through the Scriptures on having a life full of love, joy, and peace in each relational garden, as far as it depends on us. This is where the positives of the Christian life are built.

Let me clarify what I mean when I talk about righteously loving ourselves. Jesus is clear that we must love ourselves righteously if we are to love our neighbors (Matthew 22:37–39). But we are not talking about the fleshly self, which God condemns in Scripture. The fleshly self is that principle of selfishness and sin that dwells within us and is against God (Romans 8:5–8). But caring for our physical body, with its nutritional needs, need for sleep, desire for intellectual stimulation, emotional expression, and social interaction, is not sinful (Matthew 11:29; Mark 6:31; 1 Timothy 5:23). I have watched too many people overwork and neglect and abuse their bodies in the name of ministry or career advancement, and they burn out. Now they are unable to love the Lord or their neighbor, just as the Lord said. You must righteously love yourself so you can love the Lord and the people God has put in your life.

Any time I bring up this topic (Sins of Omission) with this level of clarity, it immediately becomes clear that all Christians are sinning in areas of omission every day. This is why we need the forgiveness and sacrifice of Jesus Christ all the time (1 John 1:8). We are not adequate as perfect examples of any area of our lives (2 Corinthians 3:4–5). We are hopeless, ruined sinners who Christ has redeemed through His blood. He works with us to be sanctified (set apart) from our sins and conformed to His holiness. Granted, that process will not be complete until we see Him in heaven (1 John 3:1–3), but it is our responsibility to work with Him now.

We will always be growing in overcoming the Sins of Omission. Everyone is struggling to love God as much as they should, loving their neighbors as much as they should, and loving themselves righteously as much as they should. But the more we follow Scripture, the more we feel the pleasure of God in our cooperation with Him, and also, we more readily recognize the things we fail to do in other areas.

As a personal word, this is a spiritual war. How do I fight against the World, my own Flesh, and the Devil? I build a life of love and righteousness in this broken and corrupt world. God wants to make each of us a living testimony that love, righteousness, and kindness are possible in our sin-stained world. My own life has improved so much as I have cooperated with the Lord Jesus in building it His way, not my way. I chip away at the Sins of Omission I commit by learning to love the people God has placed in my life in new ways and with greater depth—the Lord, my wife, my children, my co-workers and bosses, my friends, and the new people I meet. I am winning the spiritual war, pushing back against the darkness and showing people that God's power is stronger than the evil, selfishness, and destruction around us.

The temptations and attacks are meant to distract us from our job of loving God, loving others, and loving ourselves righteously. When we don't love as we should, we sin against God's plan for us. These Sins of Omission pave the way for the Devil, the Flesh, and the World to continue to tempt and attack us, so we will not be as loving as we should be.

SINS OF COMMISSION (TRESPASS SINS)

We can also be tempted to sin by trespassing into actions, words, and emotions we know are wrong in order to accomplish something we want, then returning to normal life as though nothing happened. These are also called Trespass Sins, or Sins of Commission, and they open the way to Zone 2 attacks, oppression, and temptations. Looking at the Ten Commandments, we certainly wouldn't want to blatantly violate what God has told us not to do. But we steal from work and then go back to our Christian lives and pretend nothing happened. It's called a Trespass Sin because we stepped across the line—we trespassed—then we got back to looking righteous without confession or repentance. We lie to protect ourselves and bear false witness against our neighbor, then pretend it was no big deal.

Trespass sins are serious because they allow the Devil to attack us and tempt us more. We commit adultery with someone who is not our spouse, or we do it online through porn, and we pretend like it's just a natural response to being human. That is a Trespass Sin, and it should be confessed and repented of, or else the Devil will get more opportunities to tempt, attack, and even oppress you as you let this "little" sin exist in your life. We go to church, but we put our sports team, our favorite celebrity, or our possessions above God in our lives. We have another god, but we pretend like we don't. This, too, is a Trespass Sin, and it needs to be confessed and repented of. When we sin, we open ourselves to more schemes of Satan. The greater level of influence of the anti-God enemies in our lives is due to Trespass Sins and Wickedness Sins.

Let's look at how these Trespass Sins can play out through the lens of the Ten Commandments:

Ten Commandments	What a Trespass Sin May Look Like:
No other gods before me.	We only put something ahead of God for a short period of time.
No graven images.	We worship some possession for a few weeks as the most important thing in our life.
No taking the name of the Lord your God in vain.	We curse and blaspheme God's name when things don't go as we want and act like it just slipped out in a moment of stress.
Remember the Sabbath Day and keep it holy.	We do not have a work/life/worship balance, and we think our crammed schedule with no time for God or rest should be able to work.
Honor your father and your mother.	We devalue our parents and the sacrifices they made. We refuse to consider them as a source of wisdom and support. We don't take care of them in their time of need.
No murder.	We get angry, even threatening violence or punching people and things to get what we want, then we pretend we were not murderously angry. We plot murder in our minds.
No adultery.	We have a quick dalliance with someone who is not our spouse or we watch dozens, if not hundreds, of adulterous actions through porn, pretending that we have not committed adultery.

Ten Commandments	What a Trespass Sin May Look Like:
No stealing.	We steal from work, from the government, or from our friends, and pretend that we have not done anything wrong.
No bearing false witness against your neighbor.	We lie to get our way or to stay out of trouble and become really good at bending the truth.
No coveting anything that belongs to your neighbor.	We don't just want things like our friends have; we want what our friends have. Often this is a person or relationship that they have.

Trespass Sins also need to be confessed, repented of, and renounced so that we do not leave a hole in our spiritual defenses. Remember, God wants you to build a righteous life of love and joy. The Devil knows that if he can get you to trespass over to the sinful side to get what you want, he has crippled you from building a solid, loving life. We will all be tempted to take shortcuts to get where and what we want, but don't do it. When the time is right, God will bless you. You can wait.

SINS OF WICKEDNESS

When people no longer even try to live by God's laws and rules, they constantly commit sins beyond the boundaries of the Ten Commandments. This is called Wickedness—Zone 3. These are people who lie constantly, steal regularly, ignore God, and even worship other gods. They use anger to get their way and violence as a regular tool in their life. They commit adultery, and they covet other people's relationships, property, and possessions. This level of sin brings a much stronger level of demonic attack, temptation, and oppression.

Wickedness brings what eventually becomes severe demonic oppression and affliction. People in this category are plagued by thoughts, feelings, and sensations that keep them locked into their sins and their lives away from God. Years ago, I was working with a man who was a convicted sex offender, and he was plagued by what he had done and the voices in his head. He was unable to attend church at the normal time with all the other Christians. For almost a year, he and I would have a private church service on Tuesday night as he confessed, repented, and renounced the things he had done. When he was cleansed completely through his prayers and the work of Jesus Christ on his soul, he could attend church without the oppression and affliction he had experienced before.

In case you're wondering whether demonic involvement still happens today, I can assure you it does. Let me share some modern examples at each level with different people I've worked with.

TRUE STORIES OF MILD DEMONIC INVOLVEMENT

A young man asked if he could see me about temptations he was facing in relation to pornography. He was regularly tempted to go to an adult bookstore on his way home from work and to indulge on the computer at home. Unfortunately, many times he listened to these temptations and exposed himself to all kinds of vile material. We had a time of confession of his sins, and I prescribed a time of fasting. I also told him to take a different way home from work, even if it added extra time to his commute. He also needed to not go on the computer after 10:00 p.m. and have his roommates hold him accountable. He won that fight with lust and developed a healthy dating relationship with a woman whom he eventually married.

I helped a lady at our church who enjoyed learning gossip and slanderous truths about others. She seemed to know every difficult or dirty thing about people and soon gained a reputation for being a gossip. People began to distrust her and didn't want to be her friend. She complained to me that our church wasn't a friendly place. After praying for her and suggesting that she be more loving to others, she came back and accused the church of not being friendly or loving.

During our meeting, I asked the Lord if I was free to tell her what I knew about her. I thought I heard a YES, so I went ahead and told her. She had a problem with gossip, and people did not want to be her friend because they knew anything they shared would be shared with everyone else in the church. She blamed other people, who just told her stuff about others. I said, "No, you are like a garbage dump. You have a huge sign on your life that says, 'I am open to all your garbage about other people and dirt on yourself.' So, people seek you out to tell you stuff about other people. They don't come and tell me all this stuff. They don't tell other people all the stuff that they tell you because they know that you want this garbage. You need to put a 'closed' sign on your garbage dump. Start telling people you no longer want to hear the difficult things about them."

After that, she was convicted in her heart that she needed to change. I asked her to pray a prayer of confession about her gossiping and interest in the sins of others. She needed to repent and find ways to love people and bless them. Sometime later, she started holding up her hand when someone was gossiping to her as if to say, "I do not want to learn this information. The garbage dump is closed."

TRUE STORIES OF MODERATE DEMONIC INVOLVEMENT

A lady who was a regular at our church was troubled

by various maladies and an almost inability to engage in spiritual depth. We came to her house and prayed over her for God's healing (James 5:16). I told her that if any particular sins came to mind while the team was praying, she should quietly confess them to the Lord as sin and tell the Lord Jesus she wanted to repent of them.

As our prayer time continued, she began praying very softly to the Lord, offering prayers of confession and repentance. The Lord appeared powerfully and healed her of the various physical ailments that had been afflicting her. She said it was like something rose up inside her and left when we were praying to confess her sins. This would be an example of a moderate level of spiritual warfare. She could go to church, yet she was blocked from a deep connection with Jesus and was plagued in various ways. Her healing and prayers of confession released God's power and drove the demonic influences away.

A man who came to our church had been unemployed for a long time. His whole family went on welfare because he could not find work. I can remember our church helping the family with meals and funds a few times. I met with him and his family at some point to pray for them. As I spent time with him, he began telling me he could find work, but not at the pay rate he wanted. He was very gifted at what he did, and he wanted to be paid at the level he felt he deserved. He was extremely proud and had an over-inflated sense of what he was worth. It seemed clear to me that God wanted him to be humble. He refused for a long time and really made himself his own god. He would decide what he should be paid, and until the world bent to his will, he would not work.

The world did not bend, so I had the privilege of praying with him about his pride. Eventually, he realized that he was putting his family through hell because of it. When he confessed that he had been prideful and repented of being unreasonable, he almost immediately got a job at a good salary.

TRUE STORIES OF SEVERE DEMONIC OPPRESSION

A woman came to see me who was struggling with severe oppression from the Devil. We cast demons out of her and worked with her for days of prayer and fasting. Only after much work did we come to understand that she had pledged an oath of loyalty to Satan if he would protect her and provide her a place to live. She was tormented by the voices and the pressure to sin in great ways. I came to realize that this was an example of dozens of people who are caught in severe bondage to the Devil. She needed to confess, repent, and renounce the oaths to Satan and the many sins she had committed so she could be free.

Another man I helped was plagued at night by his bed shaking, and he could not get any sleep. I prayed for him and with him, and we found that he knew a number of sins he was committing were wrong, but he did not want to give them up. He refused to give up his heavy use of pornography even though I pointed out to him that this was a source of his troubles. He needed to confess this habit as sin, come to Jesus Christ for deliverance, and begin the process of separating from this sexual addiction. He just wanted general prayers and help sleeping; he didn't want a radical transformation of his life. It saddens me to say that he was more in love with pornography than any sleep and inner peace.

All Christian deliverance is based on the sacrifice of Christ on the cross for our victory over the Devil. First John 1:9 is the verse that we base our prayers and cries for deliverance upon: "If we confess our sins, He is faithful and just to forgive us our sins and cleanse us of all unrighteousness." It is clear that demons cling to a person because of their sins, which can be washed away through confession, repentance, and renunciation. This is a part of cleansing us from all unrighteousness, which is what the back half of 1 John 1:9 talks about.

Confession is to agree with God that an action is wrong. If we have sinned, we need to confess our sins to the Lord to take advantage of the forgiveness and power of Christ in His death and resurrection. After we have confessed our sins, we need to repent of them, which means we head in a different direction away from the sin we confessed. Finally, we need to renounce any power or place we gave to Satan because of our participation in that sin. Second Corinthians 4:2 says it best: "but we have renounced the things hidden because of shame, not walking in craftiness or adulterating the word of God, but by the manifestation of truth commending ourselves to every man's conscience in the sight of God."

These spiritual exercises will help you develop ways to confess, repent, and renounce your sins so you can love God, others, and yourself righteously.

SPIRITUAL EXERCISES
Confess, Repent, Renounce

Confess

It is important to keep short accounts with God and allow Him to search us to see if there are any sins we are harboring that give the Devil access to our lives. I recommend doing a confession exercise daily to prevent the World, the Flesh, or the Devil from influencing us. Here are four different confession exercises that you could use.

Exercise 1—Seven Deadly Sins

As you begin praying, ask the Lord if you have committed any pride, then pause and see if He brings up any times when you have been arrogant, proud, bigoted, superior, or a know-it-all. If He brings up an incident, then agree with Him that it was wrong. Ask God to apply the blood of Christ to that sin. Tell the Lord that you want to do something different the next time you are tempted to be proud like you were. Thank Him for His forgiveness and power. Then go through the rest of the Seven Deadly Sins in the same way that you did with pride: envy, anger, lust, sloth, gluttony, and greed.

Exercise 2—Daily Bible Reading

For whatever Scripture you are reading as a part of

your devotional life, ask God if there are areas where you need to confess your sins that were brought up in that verse. Spend time agreeing with God about any areas where you missed something you should have done (Sin of Omission, where you did a little wrong to get what you wanted (Sin of Commission), or where you are just blatantly ignoring God's directions in this verse (Wickedness).

Exercise 3—Daily Sins of Omission, Commission, or Wickedness

At the end of the day, ask the Lord if you have committed any *Sins of Omission*. Have you failed to love your spouse, your family, your workmates in some way? Is there anything you could have done or should have done but didn't? Remember that this is the area of building a loving life. This is where winning the spiritual war is possible. God will always want to work with you on at least one area of your life to be a more loving, righteous, and ethical person. Listen to where He wants you to start doing one of His commands. Thankfully, He does not come after us to change everything at one time. It is usually one action at a time, one relationship at a time.

Ask the Lord if you have committed any *Sins of Commission*. Have you stepped across any of God's lines in order to get what you want and then come back like you did nothing wrong? If God brings up an incident, then agree with Him that your behavior was wrong. Ask Him what to do differently the next time that opportunity comes up. Thank Him for His love for you and draw upon His power to live righteously today.

Ask the Lord if you are committing any *Wickedness* where you are living beyond God's boundaries in some way. Does something in your life outrank God? Have you fixated on a material object as supremely important at an unhealthy level? Do you put others down and/or God for not doing things the way you would do them? Have you become a workaholic without balance between people and work, or have you become lazy and slothful? Do you regularly dishonor your God-given authorities of government, work, spouse, and/or spiritual authorities? Do you use anger or violence to get your way? Do you steal other people's property? Do you lie to get your way? Do you deeply desire the blessings, possessions, and relationships of other people? If the answer is yes, then agree with God about what He brings up. Ask Him how you can live differently. Tell God that you are giving Him power over that area of your life and taking power away from the World, the Flesh, and/or the Devil.

Exercise 4—In-Depth Confession

Pick up the book *Becoming Courageous: Facing Your Past and Building Your Future*[7] so you can go through an in-depth confession of sins that may be inviting demonic oppression, control, or bondage in your life. Ask a spiritually mature person to walk you through the chapters and exercises in this book to clean out your soul.

PRAYER
Confession

You can pray a prayer of agreement about your sins like this:

*"Lord, I **confess** that I know it was wrong when I committed adultery or stole that equipment from my work, or lied about what I did, or went to that tarot card reading, or worshipped another god, or grew deeply bitter over what happened to me, or let my anger out on my spouse and my children ... (whatever sin was committed)."*

*"I ask You to apply the blood of Christ to my sin and forgive me for my actions, words, and emotions that were wrong. Come into my life and change my life. I want to do right, but I will need Your power to act differently. I **repent** and ask that You send me in the righteous direction instead of what I did. I*

***renounce** any power or place I gave to Satan through my sin. I give You, Lord Jesus, the authority and power in my life to organize and direct my life. Thank You for dying on the cross for me. I want to grow into a godly person who lives the life You planned for me before the foundation of the world (Ephesians 2:10)."*

Each sin that God brings to mind that has not been confessed should be confessed. This process may take a while as you pray for each sin, admitting that it was wrong and not pleasing to the Lord. In this way, you are cleaning out your soul through the work of Jesus Christ's sacrifice for you. You are removing the claims that the Devil has on you. I have seen people take days, even months, as they slowly work through their confession times. This is not drudgery, but freedom. It is the spring cleaning of your soul.

I have often suggested that people find a spiritual mentor to help them with this spiritual spring cleaning. From the *Becoming Courageous* workbook I authored that helps people do this, I will often assign people to meet weekly for a year to pray through prayers of confession and build new habits of love and righteousness. This has been very helpful in removing sin and moving forward into a new Christian life, with greater sensitivity to the Lord Jesus and the Holy Spirit. I hope you will consider this resource should you need it.

Asking Jesus Christ to Become Your Savior and Your Lord

If you have never prayed a prayer of complete surrender to the Lord Jesus Christ, making Him your Lord and Savior, I would suggest praying this type of prayer before you begin any other prayers of confession. The prayer goes like this:

Dear Heavenly Father,

I come to You in the Name of the Lord Jesus Christ. I want to ask You, Lord Jesus, to be my Savior and my Lord. I realize that I am a sinner and cannot earn heaven or Your favor on my own. I believe that You, Jesus, died on the cross for my sins. I am inviting You, Jesus Christ, to be my Savior and take the punishments that I deserve. I am asking Jesus Christ to become the Lord and boss of my life. I want you, Lord Jesus, to make me the kind of person You want me to be. Thank You for dying on the cross for me. Show me how to grow as a Christian and live the new life You are offering.

In the Name of the Lord Jesus Christ,

Amen

The Three Stages of Christian Growth

There is a wonderful phenomenon exploding at many churches. Younger people are asking about spiritual warfare. How does it work? How can they defeat the Devil? What must they do to win against certain temptations? Could they learn how to cast demons out of people? How can their prayer life become deeper, more powerful, and more impactful? This is an encouraging sign because it means they are growing as Christians. They are not content to just stay in the baby stages of the Christian experience.

There have been many teachers who have suggested various stages of growth in the Christian life, but there is only one scriptural growth chart. It is given to us in 1 John 2:12–14:

> I am writing to you, little children, because your sins have been forgiven you for His name's sake. I am writing to you, fathers, because you know Him who has been from the beginning. I am writing to you, young men, because you have overcome the evil one. I have written to you, children, because you know the Father. I have written to you, fathers, because you know Him who has been from the beginning. I have written to you, young men, because you are strong, and the word of God abides in you, and you have overcome the evil one.

The apostle John, writing under the inspiration of the Holy Spirit, says there are three main stages of Christian growth: the "little children" stage, the "young man" stage, and the "father" stage. Let's dive into each stage to understand what it looks like, how to practice in it and work through it, and what your prayers could look like.

STAGE 1
Little Children

First is the little children stage or child stage. This is when you realize that your sins have been forgiven for Christ's sake and you have a relationship with God the Father through His Son, Jesus Christ. You are part of the family of God, and it is wonderful to be forgiven and to have purpose. You now have a forever family and someone who will love you.

Those who become Christians go through this stage often with great delight because of the grace, blessings, and mercy that flow into our souls. We can stay in this phase for years, just as young children are children for years.

Christians in this stage revel in the security and freedom of childhood, but they need to keep growing and recognize the consequences of sin. There is also the need to start handling the trials, tests, and even temptations that God may allow into their lives to keep them growing. Here are some ways to grow in the Christian faith when you are in this stage.

Spiritual Exercises for Christians Who Are Young in the Faith:

Let me encourage those of you who are new Christians to spend time reading about the love God has for you in the book of Ephesians and the Gospel of John. Spend time learning about the wonder of God in any and all of the gospel accounts and the deep passages about the wonder of God the Father in Romans 11 and Ephesians

1 and 3. Take the time to realize that you should long for the pure milk of the Word, as the apostle Peter tells us in 1 Peter 1.

The child stage of the Christian life is wonderful and should be nurtured with good Christian fellowship and good teaching on the wonders of the Father, the Lord Jesus, and the Holy Spirit. A good foundation of solid teaching, good fellowship, and worship on the truths of Christianity, strengthens you for the next phases of your spiritual life.

There is a negative tendency I see in some Christians where they love being a child in their faith in such a way that they do not want to ever grow beyond this childlike faith. They don't want to grapple with Christianity's more difficult issues and topics. They just want to know they are forgiven and have a relationship with the Father, who adopted them into His forever family. But the Lord wants you to continue growing up in your faith, just as a good father does not want his children to stay small but to grow into adulthood.

Pray as a Little Child in the Faith:

Dear Heavenly Father,

I come in the name of the Lord Jesus Christ. I want to know You more and understand how You want to empower me and grow me in my faith. I am so grateful for Your forgiveness of all my sins. I sense Your love and want to continue being filled up by You and Your love for me. Thank You for dying on the cross for me. Lead me to passages in Scripture that will help me understand Your sacrifice for me. Help me find Scripture and good Christian books that will explain who You are. Let me praise You accurately and worship You constantly. Guide me to great worship artists who will help me learn and sing of Your greatness. Show me the sins that You want to deal with in my life and let me change direction toward You in every case. I ask You to teach me and send me mentors who will guide me in the accurate way of the Christian faith.

In the Name of the Lord Jesus Christ,

Amen

STAGE 2
The Young Man

Let's look at the Scripture in 1 John 2:12–14 again:

> I am writing to you, little children, because your sins have been forgiven you for His name's sake. I am writing to you, fathers, because you know Him who has been from the beginning. I am writing to you, young men, because you have overcome the

evil one. I have written to you, children, because you know the Father. I have written to you, fathers, because you know Him who has been from the beginning. I have written to you, young men, because you are strong, and the word of God abides in you, and you have overcome the evil one.

There is a second stage to the Christian life where we take on the Devil and win against the temptation, deception, and oppression he has been slinging in our direction. It is like the bubble of protection is diminished, and we need to go to war with the Devil to advance in the Christian faith. I have seen many people shrink back from their faith when this happens. They didn't necessarily want to ever move beyond the easy life of a little child in the faith, but there is a time to grow up and use your spiritual muscles. I am so encouraged by those who want to win this battle that every Christian faces. This means the church has a chance to move forward and be what Jesus wanted it to be. As more people push on to maturity through the sanctification process, the world will see the church and Christians behaving like Christ in the world.

It is clear in this passage that the young-man stage involves overcoming the Evil One. This means that you have to face the areas in your life where the Devil has been winning. It means that the temptations you haven't been resisting, you will now have to start resisting. But

Scripture is clear how that can be done: strength in the Lord (Ephesians 6:10, 1 John 2:14).

To be a strong Christian, you need to have the word of God abiding in you. For forty years, I have been asking select men and women if they would like to grow deeply in their faith. It has been the profound privilege of my life to watch these young Christians grow strong in their faith and in the Word. I put them through a spiritual boot camp that takes one to three years, where they literally change because of the word of God going into them. They begin to win against the Devil. They begin to advance in their careers because of God's work in them. They begin to build deep, loving relationships through the wisdom of the Holy Spirit and their obedience to His promptings.

It is this training process that thrusts them into spiritual warfare. It is the spiritual warfare that convinces them that life is real and the battles can be brutal. They watch as some people confess, repent, and make progress in their lives, marriages, finances, and careers. Others won't admit that their sins are all that bad, and they remain plagued by the consequences of their repeated sins and by the flaming arrows of the World, the Flesh, and the Devil. Christians who want to grow will win some battles against the enemies of their Christian faith, but they will lose others. What matters is whether they get up and keep fighting. The apostle Paul says it this way in Philippians 2:12–13:

> So then, my beloved, just as you have always obeyed, not as in my presence only, but now much more in my absence, work out your salvation with fear and trembling; for it is God who is at work in you, both to will and to work for His good pleasure.

The struggle against sin and the work of the Devil is a noble endeavor. But we must do it in the power of the Lord with His armor of truth, righteousness, and the gospel of peace firmly on at all times. We take up God's armor in the times of intense fighting for ourselves and for others, with faith, salvation, the word of God, prayer, and alertness to the schemes of Satan (Ephesians 6:10–18).

I have watched many young men and women powerfully engage to help others and themselves escape the Devil's clutches. This is what we need. Sometimes, as they fight the Devil and their own temptations, they can forget the first lesson we discussed in this basic spiritual warfare book: *to become better lovers of the Lord, others, and themselves.* Sometimes they can be so consumed with hating and fighting the Devil that they sling truth at others without any love. Remember that during the young-man stage, Jesus's new commandment still applies: "A new commandment I give unto you that you love one another as I have loved you."

Spiritual Exercises for the Young Man

My call to all believers is to go after deeper Christian growth. Learn the Spiritual Disciplines or Spiritual Exercises. I recommend my book, *Spiritual Disciplines of a C.H.R.I.S.T.I.A.N.*,[8] which I have been using to help people grow during this young-man stage. Learn how to practice your faith through confession, listening to the promptings of the Holy Spirit, meditation on Scripture, doing Bible study and prayer at deeper levels, serving God and His people in daily, gifted, and fruitful ways, worshipping God deeply with or without music, finding a helpful fellowshipping community of Christians, identifying with Christ through baptism, communion, and witnessing, learning how to intensify your prayers through abstinence, and meeting needs at new levels in your daily life through generosity. For thousands of years, this is how Christian disciples have grown into and through this young-man stage.

For further reading in this critical area, read *Celebration of Discipline* by Richard Foster and many other excellent books and videos on the Spiritual Exercises. I also have online courses on Udemy.com that will help you grow, including *Spiritual Disciplines of the Christian Life, Mission Possible: Winning the Battle over Sexual Temptation, and The Keys to Grapeness: Growing a Spirit-Led Life*.

Pray as the Young Man:

Dear Heavenly Father,

I come in the name of the Lord Jesus Christ. I ask You to strengthen me in my faith. I want to be strong spiritually and in the power of Your might. Teach me how to practice the Spiritual Disciplines so I can overcome the Devil and the sins that have beaten me in the past. I know that I will face many battles, some I will win and some I will lose. Don't let me get discouraged, but remind me to ask You to fill me again and find a way to battle until I live in righteous love. I need You to help me consider all of the tests and trials I will face as joyful ways to strengthen me for the life You have planned for me. I ask You to help me abide in the word of God and strengthen me through the life that is embedded in the Scriptures. Show me the sins that are damaging and destroying my future. Show me how I can help others in their battle with the World, the Flesh, and the Devil. I ask that You, Lord Jesus, would strengthen me, guide me, and give me wisdom that I don't currently have to go through this essential second stage of the Christian life.

In the Name of the Lord Jesus Christ,

Amen

STAGE 3
The Father

Let's look again at these crucial verses in 1 John 2:12–14 to see what God is telling us about this final stage of the Christian life:

> I am writing to you, little children, because your sins have been forgiven you for His name's sake. I am writing to you, fathers, because you know Him who has been from the beginning. I am writing to you, young men, because you have overcome the evil one. I have written to you, children, because you know the Father. I have written to you, fathers, because you know Him who has been from the beginning. I have written to you, young men, because you are strong, and the word of God abides in you, and you have overcome the evil one.

The final stage is what God calls the "Father" stage. This stage is when you have walked with God enough that you understand Him as the Ancient of Days. He is still your Father, but you are aware of the vastness and power and majesty of God. You willingly submit to the wonder and goodness of God. We read John the Apostle write about this stage in First, Second, and Third John, as well as in the book of Revelation. God was everything to John. He walked with Jesus, he raised up churches throughout Asia Minor, he was given visions of the end of the world, and he focused on God, the One who was before all creation and will be there in the end at the New Heavens and the New Earth.

There is still growth in this final stage as you constantly learn more about God. But you are settled in your faith in a way that was probably not the case in earlier years. As Polycarp, who was discipled by John the Apostle, said when he was facing martyrdom in his old age, "Eighty-six years I have served him, and he never did me any injury; how then can I blaspheme my King and my Savior?"[9] Polycarp was a father in the faith, as evidenced by his undying commitment to his Lord and Savior.

In this final phase of your Christian life, you will have read the Scriptures many times. You will have discussed and even debated various views on crucial doctrines and have settled biblical opinions on who God is, on who Jesus is and what He has done, on the Holy Spirit, on the inspiration and inerrancy of the Bible, on the wonder of God's love in salvation, on the gift of the church to humanity, on the afterlife, and on the return of Christ. You are more in love with God the Father, God the Son, and God the Holy Spirit, and more settled in Him. You are waiting to be taken to Him in the next world. You live and serve at God's direction.

Your prayer life is your life. Everything is run by and through the Lord Jesus Christ. You realize that He is in charge and you are not. You want to please Him with every choice you make. You want to use your gifts, abilities, life, and resources to advance His causes and His Kingdom. You are aware of His love for you and the many blessings He has bestowed on you. But there is always room to grow, as we will never be perfect or have all the knowledge here on earth.

Spiritual Exercises for the Father Stage

There are so many good books and resources that help a Christian grow. Take the time to read some of the Christian classics from believers who have walked with God for a long time. Eugene Peterson's insights in *A Long Obedience* are valuable here. A.W. Tozer and his insights on *The Pursuit of God and The Attributes of God*. *The Christian's Secret of a Happy Life* by Hannah Whitall Smith, *Knowing God* by J.I. Packer, and *Mere Christianity* by C.S. Lewis are other terrific books. Read the biographies of Christian godly men and women like Hudson Taylor, George Müller, and Theresa of Avila. I can also recommend my book Developing a Christian Worldview to get you started in the Scriptures on these broad but crucial doctrinal points.

As I trained pastors throughout much of my career, I was surprised by how many future pastors did not have the basic doctrinal foundations of Scripture in their heads, so they could not advance to this Father stage. I've provided you with some valuable resources to start with, and I hope you will use them to keep growing in your faith.

Pray as a father in the faith:

Dear Heavenly Father,

I come in the name of the Lord Jesus Christ to surrender to You, God the Father, God the Son, and God the Holy Spirit. I want to know You at a new level, just as Paul sought to know You in the depth of Your resurrection and the power of Your suffering. Show me new depths of who You are as the Ancient of Days. Show me more from Your Word about Your work, Lord Jesus, on this earth. Guide me, Holy Spirit, into a clearer understanding of how You want to work in my life and through my life. Help me to see and be attracted to new depths in Your Word. Let me explore the wonders of Your love for me and those who will inherit salvation from before creation to the introduction of the New Heavens and the New Earth.

Empower me to help the church become all it can be in my lifetime. Let me revel in new insights about my life with You in the next life. Give me insights and anticipation for Your return, Lord Jesus. May my life be a living testimony of what You did for and through a sinner like me. I give You praise, Lord Jesus, and ask that I would know You at new depths until I see You face to face. I pray that I may serve You in this world and the next one to Your glory and praise.

In the Name of the Lord Jesus Christ,

Amen

ROUND 4

Understanding Enemy #1: The World

There is a wonderful phenomenon exploding at many churches. Younger people are asking about spiritual warfare. How does it work? How can they defeat the Devil? What must they do to win against certain temptations? Could they learn how to cast demons out of people? How can their prayer life become deeper, more powerful, and more impactful? This is an encouraging sign because it means they are growing as Christians. They are not content to just stay in the baby stages of the Christian experience.

Unfortunately, our psychological age has convinced us that the only thoughts in our heads must come from within. But a proper spiritual understanding of the World tells us there are other thoughts and feelings originating from other sources that can pass through our souls. Destructive and negative thoughts, choices, and emotions that are truly foreign to our best interests are actually spiritual attacks. Luckily, we don't have to latch onto them or embrace them as our own. We can fight back.

We need to understand that the spiritual war we are fighting is trying to rob us of the love we should have shown (Sins of Omission), tempt us to gain at another's loss (Sins of Commission), and involve us in soul-destroying activities that will imprison us (Wickedness). God, however, has a great plan for our lives, one that is full of loving relationships and blessings (John 10:10). But we must be active in choosing to use the gifts, blessings, and benefits that He has given us in Christ.

The first step in winning at spiritual warfare is understanding our enemies and the tactics they use against us. Christians face three spiritual enemies that originate from three very different places. Each of them, in their own way, can fire invisible, destructive thoughts, choices, and feelings at us to keep us from the good we could do. Long term, these enemies want to rob us of the righteous lives we could enjoy. We are fortunate because the Scriptures tell us the names of our enemies and how they seek to derail us (tactics); most importantly, Scripture also tells us how to defeat them. Let's take a look.

The first spiritual enemy is called the World (1 John 2:15–17). This is the cultural, political, and local ways of thinking that conceal God's will and get us to chase after stupid trophies and foolish rewards. The World System wants us to spend our lives pursuing anything but God and righteousness. It wants us to give up the pursuit of God and His righteous ways and instead to clamor for the approval of others and for some insignificant goal. Our world makes a very big deal about winning a ring in football, a statue for acting, or a corner office for selling the most sugar water. It wants us to pay the most attention to what it wants and values, rather than what God wants and values.

The arrows that the World will fire at your soul are cultural desires. Our Enemy wants us to win in the eyes of everyone we know. These endeavors will feel like the right things to go after, but they won't be pleasing to God, just like we can see someone and ask, "Why are they dressed like that?" "Why do they act like that?" "Why do they like that activity?" All of these behaviors and patterns are to please some group or individuals. The messages are sometimes subtle, like "Don't you want this?" These arrows are designed to move us toward a false goal, so we will miss God's best for our lives.

Let's read one of the most powerful passages on the World as an enemy:

> Do not love the world nor the things in the world. If anyone loves the world, the love of the Father is not in him. For all that is in the world, the lust of the flesh and the lust of the eyes and the boastful pride of life, is not from the Father, but is from the world. The world is passing away, and also its lusts; but the one who does the will of God lives forever. (1 John 2:15–17)

Right now, your culture, social media, TV programs, and movies are trying to sell you something that is not true. They have an agenda that they hope you will adopt, like "Sex is always good if you feel something for the person." "Being a rebel is cool if the people are older than you." "There are many pathways to God and meaning in life." "Lying is something that everyone does, so it is okay." "Stealing from a corporation or rich person is not wrong if they are rich." The World System wants you to adapt to its system of good and bad, right and wrong. It wants you to chase after money, power, fame, and prestige. It is very easy to feel that doing what God says in the Bible is old-fashioned or stupid, while the latest fad or modern point of view is best. These are the temptations of the World.

The World as a spiritual enemy consists of the messages around you that tell you what is good, acceptable, and popular, which is different from what God and His Word are telling you. The World is lying to you. It wants you to embrace a value, a lifestyle, or a way of thinking that is destructive to you, others, and/or society as a whole.

The World System is the unexamined answers to your Google searches and your YouTube viewing. They are pushing a self-focused point of view. So we need to ask, "Is it godly, biblical, and righteous?" Stop asking value, meaning, and wisdom questions of TikTok, ChatGPT, Google, and YouTube, and start asking the Bible about these deeper questions of life. The World System, or your cultural system, wants you to look to its answers to meet your needs, pursue you, and please you. It doesn't tell you that no one wins, or very few win, at the lifestyle it is pushing. The number of aspiring actors who actually make it is very small, but the number of actors who make it and get addicted to drugs, alcohol, fame, greed, and the like is very large. The same story goes for the sports stars who look so appealing. The World System that you are tempted to chase will leave you lonely and alone, not knowing who to trust. We have all known people who got stuck in a fad hairstyle, job, clothing style, or social life that no longer is the "in" thing. But they still see themselves as the cool person of some decade.

I had a friend who got caught up in the party scene at the end of high school. He was one of the cool people, he believed, because he got invited to all the high school parties. He smoked the dope, he went with the girls, he drove the cool car. Ten years later, he woke up in the middle of a party, realizing that he was twenty-seven and everyone else was seventeen. He had missed out on college and a stable career path. He needed to reject the temptations of the World and begin to listen to God. He repented and followed the Lord for a few years, but the pull of the World was so strong that he went back to partying with slightly older people, got cool again, and went nowhere with his life.

SPIRITUAL EXERCISES
Three Pathways of Worldly Temptation

In what ways are social media, movies, television, friends, and your culture causing you to approve of what God doesn't approve of or to hate what God loves? Let's examine the three pathways of temptation that the World System presents to us from Scripture: the lust of the flesh, the lust of the eyes, and the boastful pride of life.

The Three Temptations of the World
Lust of the Flesh - Lust of the Eyes - Boastful Pride of Life

The Lust of the Flesh:

The World System ties into the selfish and sinful desires of the flesh. The early church created a shorthand list of the sins and temptations of the flesh so the Christian could know when they are being tempted by the World using the flesh. They called them the Seven Deadly Sins: Pride, Envy, Anger, Lust, Sloth, Gluttony, and Greed. The World knows that we are susceptible to some of these directions and uses that knowledge to lure you into throwing away hours, days, weeks, and years of your life chasing things that will not reward you as they promise.

I recommend that people use the Seven Deadly Sins as a daily confession guide, so they can let God search their lives for when they have been tempted and/or given in to one of them. Remember, there will be some of these that do not tempt you, but others that are very powerful in their pull toward sin and selfishness. Let God point out where you need to confess. Don't try to be a perfectionist or try to find something under each sin if you aren't tempted or attacked in that area. Move along and allow God to make you ready to win against the World Systems' use of the lust of the flesh.

EXTENDED WORKOUT
The Seven Deadly Sins

I often use the list of the Seven Deadly Sins as a quick reference for what the selfish urges inside me might prompt me to do. These seven sins are pride, envy, anger, lust, sloth, gluttony, and greed. Here is an expanded understanding of these categories of sin. As you read this list, realize that inside of you is a distorted version of yourself that wants to twist you in the direction of one to three of these sins. Your job as a Christian is to die to those sins (crucify yourself) and live a life of wisdom and power in the Holy Spirit, being the opposite of these selfish impulses. There are some of these that regularly attack you, and some that you rarely, if ever, feel. Focus on the ones that you regularly feel prompted by.

1. Read each sin aloud slowly, including its definition. Let God prompt you about the sins that concern you:

Pride: Inordinate self-esteem; showing feelings of superiority; unwillingness to submit (rebellion);

self-absorption; overbearing; lack of teachability; desire or demand for supremacy.

Envy: Desire for what belongs to another; being consumed by the unfairness of another's material possessions; desire to deprive others of what they have or could have; the feeling of displeasure at another's benefit; inability to rejoice with another's benefit without desiring it personally.

Anger: Selfishness expressed forcefully outward; being blocked from a goal; unwillingness to surrender a "right"; irritated; seething; vengeful; plotting against. Anger also includes bitterness and rebellion, as they grow out of anger.

Lust: Strong/inordinate sexual desire; inability to interact with another person without sexual thoughts or innuendo; sexual desire for someone other than your spouse; constant sexual thoughts.

Sloth: Laziness; working with a minimum effort; procrastination; delaying crucial decisions; inordinate attention to insignificant things; unwillingness to do things completely.

Gluttony: Overindulgence in a physical pleasure; addictive behavior; seeking comfort, solace, escape in a physical pleasure; moving past moderation in anything.

Greed: Longing after money; evaluating all things in terms of the money that can be made or lost; pursuing money above other, more important things; seeking in and through money the comfort, pleasure, security, and intimacy that comes from God.

2. Go back through each definition and dwell on its meaning. Jot down notes or key thoughts that come to mind.

3. Ask yourself the following questions: Is this true of me? In what ways have I committed this sin? Am I moving close to committing this sin? *Caution: Do not try to find violations just because you think there should be some.*

4. When you begin to see the ways that you have transgressed God's command, confess them to God, admitting that it is wrong. It is not uncommon, and is usually desirable, to weep and mourn (James 4:7–10); it's okay to cry. It can be helpful to picture yourself doing the offense and watching God's reaction of grief, holy anger, sadness, etc.

5. Write down situations you need to clear up because of your involvement in one of the Seven Deadly Sins.

6. Accept God's forgiveness in Christ by acknowledging your need for Christ's payment on the cross for you. Thank Him for His forgiveness and love for you (see Jeremiah 31:34; Zechariah 13:1; Isaiah 53:6;

John 1:29; 1 Peter 2:24,25). It can be very helpful to picture yourself at the foot of the cross, admitting to Christ that you are guilty of (name the sin).

7. Ask God the Holy Spirit to empower you to keep away from this sin. Picture yourself doing what would please God in each of these seven areas: Humility, Understanding, Caring, Flexibility, Meekness, Purity, Diligence, Moderation, Generosity. Think through every part of tomorrow in your mind and see yourself acting righteously, and not being prideful, envious, angry, lustful, slothful, gluttonous, or greedy. Take your time and go through each sin individually and picture yourself acting in the opposite way.[10]

The table below contrasts the Seven Deadly Sins and their positive counterparts.[11]

Deadly Sin:	Opposite of the Sin:
Pride	Humility, Teachability, Gratefulness
Envy	Contentment, Charity, Zeal for the Lord
Anger	Meekness, Forgiveness, Power Under Control
Lust	Purity, Righteous Desire
Sloth	Diligence, Hard work, Efficiency
Gluttony	Mourning, Moderation
Greed	Generosity, Wisdom

The World wants to use your natural orientation toward a few of these temptations to lead you away from a life of righteousness and love. So often, we watch people who were excited about the Lord Jesus get caught up in the cares of the World and lose sight of following Christ. This is just what Jesus said would happen to some would-be disciples in the Parable of the Sower in Matthew 13.

The Lust of the Eyes

The apostle John points out that the World System, our current culture, and even our subculture, are very focused on what people see. We are often tempted most by what we see around us. We want to fit in. We want to have what others have. We see the apple and realize it is good for food, as Eve did in the Garden of Eden. This fixation on what we see, what is beautiful, and what is desirable lures us toward what is damaging to righteous love. Notice that advertisers never put ugly models on billboards or TV. What are your eyes beginning to fixate on? Is it a material possession? Is it a person? Is it a job? Is it a certain lifestyle you have seen or are watching? We all want to grow and do better in our lives, but we must also balance that with gratitude for what we have and contentment with what we already have. The World System never wants you to be grateful or content. It wants you to go after what you see as soon as you realize you want it.

Ask yourself, What is the World System putting in front of me, hoping I will desire it because it's something I see regularly?

The Boastful Pride of Life:

The apostle John, speaking under the inspiration of the Holy Spirit, says that one of the ways that the World will try and lure us is through boastful pride. It is amazing, but everyone seems to have an ego that can be deflated to low or inflated to high. It is this unhealthy level of ego that causes the problems. The World around us wants us to feel like we are nothing if we aren't the right height, weight, dressed in the right clothes, or doing the cool thing. The World also wants us to feel like we are the kings of the world because we did well on a sports field, won a beauty contest, have more money than someone else, or live in a different part of town. Remember, the World wants to either remind you that you are nothing and not worthy or that everything and everybody should pay attention to you or do things your way. The apostle Paul weighs in on this temptation from the World in Romans 12:3

> For through the grace given to me I say to everyone among you not to think more highly of himself than he ought to think; but to think so as to have sound judgment, as God has allotted to each a measure of faith.

Real Humility
—What Does Healthy Self-Respect Look Like?
"For through the grace given to me I say to everyone among you not to think more highly of himself than he ought to think; but to think so as to have sound judgment, as God has allotted to each a measure of faith." (Rom. 12:3-4)

How are you being tempted by the World in this boastful pride category? Are you being tempted to think too little of yourself, or are you sliding in the direction of thinking too much of yourself? Aim for the Love of God to envelop you, allowing you to have healthy self-respect.

PRAYER
The World's Influence

Dear Heavenly Father,

I come in the name of the Lord Jesus Christ and ask You to show me the ways that the World System is distorting the truth of what is good, acceptable, and right. Help me recognize how my thinking is being attacked by stories, ideas, and arguments that seek to approve what God has declared destructive. Help me realize how doing these things outside of God's boundaries will damage, if not kill, my righteous love for the people in my life. Fill me with Your Spirit so I can be a loving, joyful, peaceful, and patient person, full of kindness, goodness, meekness, faithfulness, and self-control. A great life is waiting for me to seize it through Your power and wisdom. Show me how to do this.

In the Name of the Lord Jesus Christ,

Amen

Weapon #1: Do Not Love the World

To understand the weapon that God has fashioned against the World, you must first understand love. Love means meeting needs, pursuing, and pleasing. God tells us that the greatest weapon to defeat the mental and emotional lies that the World will weave in your mind is to not love the World System, and most importantly, your world system. In other words, don't pursue it, don't try to please it, and don't meet its needs.

John 2:15–17, God tells us that the World wants us to completely embrace its ways of thinking and values and to pursue its forms of success. But if we do that, we will miss God's best. Your culture and subculture are trying to weave a tale of woe that will keep you away from God. You'll make little positive impact as you keep yourself busy with your "duties, interests, and pursuits."

I remember having dinner with a man in his seventies when I was in my early twenties. He described the great life he enjoyed serving God. He had become a Christian late in his teens and was then called to the mission field. He told us about how he had traveled the world and helped all kinds of people spiritually, physically, medically, emotionally, and psychologically. He had friends literally all over the world. When he was in his sixties, he went back to the town where he grew up. All of his old friends were there, the ones who had told him he was a fool to be a missionary, giving up his business abilities to serve God. Then he began to regale them with stories of his life, all the places he had visited, all the friends he had made, and how his life had impacted others. It became apparent to them that he was no fool to follow God's path. Their safe lives spent piling up money had led them to miss many of life's wonders. As I write this, I am seventy years old, and I know firsthand that he is right. Serving God in whatever way He asks brings about the best life.

WEAPON #1: DO NOT LOVE THE WORLD

All of us live in a subculture that may or may not be righteous in its outlook on life. Consider the gang culture in many cities in America. This subculture believes that selling drugs is good, murdering rival gang members is good, and protecting their leaders and members from the police is good. From a Christian point of view, all of these behaviors are bad, but from within that subculture, they are good.

Think of a racist subculture that says only people of your own skin color are good and people of a different skin color are bad. We can think of certain business subcultures where any means of making money is acceptable, even if it means lying, stealing, cheating, or harming people. As long as a healthy profit is made, it's good!

Certain nationalistic subcultures exist where anything done for the nation is good, and anything that puts the nation in an unfavorable light is bad. In some cases, it can lead to justifying torture, endorsing sex crimes, and approving payments to murderers. In many high schools, a subculture exists in which popularity is the highest prize, and social media tools are used to destroy classmates to promote one's own popularity. It's possible for any subculture to embrace evil as good and good as evil.

If we are good at our subculture and "winning" at its values, we will end up loving those values. God tells us not to love our subculture but to love Him and His moral structure. Don't be sucked in by messages of your subculture when what it is telling you is not biblical. I almost missed one of the greatest blessings of my life this way. When I met the woman who became my wife, I was instantly drawn to her beauty, wisdom, charm, and spirituality. But I was raised in intellectual and philosophical circles that loved to debate abstract ideas. This was one of my highest values. I just enjoyed philosophizing about all kinds of theories and ideas. I did it at every level of education, and I went halfway around the world to do it with intellectuals in Switzerland. It was so much fun and so personally satisfying.

But after dating this amazing woman, I found that she did not like philosophizing. In fact, she told me that she did not do it and would not learn to do it. I was crushed and realized I would need to break up with her because this was such a big part of who I was and what I wanted my life to be about. The morning that I was going to break up with her, I was reading in my devotions about wisdom in Proverbs, and the Scriptures said, "Wisdom is more valuable than jewels, and nothing you desire is more important than her." I knew God was talking to me about Dana. "But she doesn't philosophize," I argued. I heard a question back, "But is she wise?" "Yes," I replied. "She is extremely wise and spiritually very godly." Then I heard Him answer,

"Then you have your answer; you are wrong." I began to cry and confess my sin that I had elevated philosophizing above wisdom and godliness. I had listened to my subcultural definition of the perfect mate.

That day, I repented and moved forward with the process of asking her to marry me. She has been the best friend I have ever had. I could not do what I do without her. She has been comforting, encouraging, even confrontive at times, and a constant source of support and prayer. I almost missed God's best because I had been a dupe of the World System I grew up in. Do not love the World, but do love God with all your heart, soul, mind, and strength.

Right now, your subculture is trying to get you to be okay with something that God says is not okay. How do we know whether something is okay or not? By looking at an objective standard that does not change. Cultures change and seek to change the rules of morality, but God's morality never changes. When someone has to lose in order for another person to win, that's when you know it is wrong.

The Ten Commandments are an outline of God's unalterable standards of morality; I invite you to read and memorize them (Exodus 20:1–17):

THE TEN COMMANDMENTS

You shall have no other gods before Me.

You shall not make for yourself any graven images.

You shall not take the name of the LORD your God in vain.

Remember the sabbath day, to keep it holy.

Honor your father and your mother.

You shall not murder.

You shall not commit adultery.

You shall not steal.

You shall not bear false witness against your neighbor.

You shall not covet anything that belongs to your neighbor.

When you read through these commandments, does your subculture suggest approval of ways to harm people that go against them?

What message is your subculture sending that is not godly, according to these commandments?

God further tells us how to successfully win against conforming to our subculture. It is clear from Matthew

6:33 that the Christian is to have other goals: "But seek first His kingdom and His righteousness, and all these things will be added to you." It is God and His righteousness that we are to pursue, and His Love—not the values, trophies, and goals of the World. This is the weapon that clears away the fog of our subculture's misdirection. We must regularly ask, "How do I love God and love righteousness in my world?" "Why am I doing what I am doing?" "Does what I am putting my time, energy, and resources into actually promote God's goals, God's righteousness, and God's redemptive purposes?"

I know a business leader who, in the midst of making a profit, was able to also provide jobs and funding for ending the injustice of human trafficking. This really made a difference on a number of levels. If employers can provide decent jobs with reasonable pay and benefits, they are providing a righteous element in their communities. God continues to prompt teachers, businesspeople, doctors, politicians, lawyers, police, and hundreds of other occupations to use the power of their vocation for righteousness in ways that haven't been done yet. They will not necessarily maximize their profits, but they will be conforming to God's ideas.

When you find yourself loving the perks of your subculture a little too much, then look out—you are being deceived. When you find yourself pushing really hard to be noticed in some cultural way, realize that this is "loving the World," and you are already being deceived. When you find yourself being overly pleased by some stupid cultural pleasure, you are being lured into a love relationship with that cultural pleasure. It is not that we cannot enjoy the world we live in, but we cannot let it latch its claws on us so that we do what it wants above other, more important things.

God has shown each of us injustices we could fight against. He has given us several ways to pursue a deeper relationship with Him. He has given us ways to promote righteous and good things. Be in love with pushing toward these things. The World hates it when you don't think in lockstep with your subculture, but breaking free from the deception of your subculture brings great freedom.

SPIRITUAL EXERCISE
Seek First the Kingdom of God

The essential weapon to defeat the World Systems' spiritual attacks against your soul is "Do not love the world or the things in the world." Do not seek the World's pleasures and answers to meet your needs, soothe your soul, or please you. They only work temporarily. We have to be willing to not adapt to the culture around us in various ways.

We also need to avoid clamoring for the approval and encouragement of a groupthink that is not in line with God's thinking. Sometimes this involves doing things with different priorities, like spending time with our family instead of chasing every last dollar in our business or professional world. Sometimes it means we will not indulge in something pleasurable because it harms others. Sometimes it means that we refuse to support an organization or political candidate because they approve something that is immoral or cruel. Sometimes it means that we do not spend as much time with something or someone that is easy to become overinvolved with or consumed by. The World System doesn't care what you are consumed with as long as it is not loving God and important people in your life.

Go after God's plan, God's pleasures, and God's relationships. While we do not let the World System meet our needs or become our life goals, we do need goals. God told us what those goals should be: loving God with all your heart, soul, mind, and strength, and your neighbor as yourself. There is a myriad of pleasures within God's boundaries that excite our hearts and fill our lives with meaning. Go after these; don't get caught up in trying to be pleasing to the anti-God culture around you. Jesus provided the positive side of the "Do Not Love the World" weapon when He said, "Seek ye first the kingdom of God and all these other things will be added to you" (Matthew 6:33). Too many people think that God is all about the NO, but this is not true. God is about the right YES—the righteous yes. So go after God's beauty and love and relationships and accomplishments with all the energy and wisdom He has given you. To do that, you have to say NO to the faddish, harmful, and unproductive ideas of parts of the culture around you.

PRAYER
New Paths, New People, and New Experiences

Dear Heavenly Father,

I come in the Name of the Lord Jesus Christ, asking You to show me where the World System is trying to get me to wait for the approval, love, and support of the World. Give me the power and wisdom to turn away from these false ideas and relationships and to turn instead to the relationships and connection to You, Lord. Open my eyes to see the new paths, new people, and new experiences that You have waiting for me. Give me the energy to go after the full life You have laid out for me. I thank You that I am Your workmanship, created in Christ Jesus, where You have all kinds of good works and adventures for me to explore (Ephesians 2:10).

In the Name of the Lord Jesus Christ,

Amen

Understanding Enemy #2: The Flesh

The second spiritual enemy is the Flesh. Scripture tells us that the Flesh consists of the impulses, desires, and temptations to indulge ourselves beyond what is healthy and righteous. The apostle Paul described it this way in Romans 6:11–14:

> Even so consider yourselves to be dead to sin, but alive to God in Christ Jesus. Therefore do not let sin reign in your mortal body so that you obey its lusts, and do not go on presenting the members of your body to sin as instruments of unrigh-

teousness; but present yourselves to God as those alive from the dead, and your members as instruments of righteousness to God. For sin shall not be master over you, for you are not under law but under grace.

Living within us, we have a principle of selfishness and personal pleasure. This "thing" within us is sinful, rebellious, and pleasure-seeking. The Flesh wants to be in charge of your thought life, your words, your emotions, and your actions. It is trying to create a version of you that is not righteous, loving, or kind. The Flesh wants us to say everything we think to others. It wants us to give in to every desire we have. It wants our hormones to rule our lives. It wants our base instincts to lead us. It wants us to embrace irritation and express our anger when things don't go our way. It wants us to focus on ourselves and push for what we want in every situation. It wants us to live for the moment, giving no thought to the future, the relationship, or the next life.

The arrows of the Flesh are the selfish urges coming from inside of you, directed at your soul. There is a selfish, demanding two-year-old inside of you who wants its way no matter what. It will continue to pitch a fit until it gets what it wants unless you recognize it for the enemy it is and overcome its urges, what the Bible refers to as "dying to self":

> So then, brethren, we are under obligation, not to the flesh, to live according to the flesh—for if you are living according to the flesh, you must die; but if by the Spirit you are putting to death the deeds of the body, you will live. (Romans 8:12–13)

What many people don't realize is that this principle of selfishness and sin is not the real us. In many cases, it has been in charge so long that we believe it is our authentic self, but it isn't. It is an alternative version of us that keeps us imprisoned in bad relationships, selfish actions, get-rich-quick schemes, and depressive thoughts.

This particular enemy, the Flesh, wants to encase the real you in so many layers of sin and selfishness that few people ever see the kind, authentic self that you are. You may not even recognize that version of yourself, but you can change, and I'll show you how.

SPIRITUAL EXERCISE
Recognize What Deeds of the Flesh Are Tempting to You

Galatians 5 lists fleshly sins. Take a look at the Scripture below and see which ones you are tempted to engage in.

> Now the deeds of the flesh are evident, which are: immorality, impurity, sensuality, idolatry, sorcery, enmities, strife, jealousy, outbursts of

anger, disputes, dissensions, factions, envying, drunkenness, carousing, and things like these …" (Galatians 5:19–21)

Go back and circle the ones you have felt compelled to do from time to time. You will not be tempted to do all of them, but a few of them will be your go-to desires.

You will most likely find a few things in the expanded list below that you feel tempted to do. This is what this enemy, the Flesh, wants to do—gum up the works of your life so you don't live a loving, righteous life. This principle of selfishness and sin inside of you is capable of many things and wants to push you so deeply into your pleasures and sins that you don't think you can retreat.

> **Immorality:** Moving beyond the moral boundaries of the Ten Commandments. This is promoting something other than God to prime importance or worshipping other gods, blasphemy, work/life/worship balance, rebellion from God-given authorities, anger, threats of violence, violence, sexual activity outside of marriage, stealing, lying, coveting the things, people, and possessions of your neighbor.
>
> **Impurity:** Being involved with activities and mental images that require harm to others or degrading yourself or others in some way.

Sensuality: Increasing sexualization before, during, and after marriage to people and practices beyond your marriage, whether that is pornography or perversion.

Idolatry: Putting something physical or spiritual in the place of God. This can be money, an idol, or another god.

Sorcery: This means using spiritual means to gain the power of others and things. It is in the original word pharmakia … which is where we get our word pharmacy from. This type of selfishness usually involves drugs, alcohol, and other mind-altering substances to change your perception or to move you into false spirituality that may change others' actions.

Enmities: This is hatred, bigotry, and resentment that carry on between you and another person or you and a group. Your flesh urges you to have people you hate so much that you can't see their humanity.

Strife: This is starting a disagreement or a fight with another person. It can be short-term or long-term, but it causes tension between you and the other person. Some people have adopted this part of the flesh so much that they cannot stand peace and quiet, so they pick a fight or start drama if things are going too well. I remember one woman who didn't like it when her husband and she got along too well, so she would pick a fight with him just to keep things tense.

Jealousy: This is the sin of comparison, where you have something, and you become consumed by keeping others from having what you have. This is the husband who is very jealous of his wife and doesn't want her to talk to anyone. This is the woman who has a beautiful dress or coat and becomes incensed when anyone else has it.

Outbursts of anger: This is where your anger, rage, or hatred comes pouring out of your body through speech, actions, attitudes, and gestures. In this way, the Flesh wants to encase the person in an angry persona. Others will not want to approach because they fear this person's angry outbursts or rude comments.

Disputes: This is where your flesh can never let anything go. You cannot be wrong. You cannot in any way be taken advantage of. You must fight about everything. You seem to enjoy fighting over a word, a gesture, a statement made years ago, or a few dollars. This person's persona is that they fight about everything, so others do not tell them or bring things up to them because it will start a fight.

Dissensions: This is the deeper principle of fighting, where people stop talking to one another because they don't want to fight; they want to win and be proved right. This temptation causes family members to stop talking to each other. I hear people say, "We don't talk to them!" many times. When you ask what they are all upset about, it is usually something that happened years ago, or sometimes they don't even remember, but they are the bad people.

Factions: This is the deepest level of fighting and dissensions. This is where groups are being rallied to the cause of not interacting with other groups. We see this racially, culturally, in class warfare, and in many other groups. This temptation wants you to believe that you are superior to that group, or you are the victim of that group, or you don't have anything in common with that group. This will shut you off from many good people and different perspectives.

Envying: This is the selfish practice of comparing yourself to others over what they have that you don't. This sinful practice wants you to think bad thoughts about the possessions of others and how they obtained them. Some people are driven by this form of coveting and must have whatever others have. It is keeping up with the Joneses. Don't fall for this temptation, for it will destroy your bank account and your soul.

Drunkenness: This is the selfish pursuit of alcohol or drugs to make some emotional pain go away. This is a false solution to deep emotional hurt. There is usually some deep hurt that moves a person toward regular drunkenness. In this way, it traps people in a pseudo-solution that won't work long term. It wants you to use this behavior to mask what is really going on, so you will destroy parts of your life.

Carousing: This is the party temptation. Maybe by going to enough parties, you can escape the reality of your life and its problems. In this way, the selfish principle in you wants you to be busier and busier "having a good time" so you don't notice that you are not building a real, loving life.

These are the ways the Flesh will try and keep you from being loving. When you should say something loving, you will be tempted to say something sarcastic. When you should be willing to lose a game or argument out of meekness and humility, you will be tempted to rage in a different direction or accuse the other person of cheating or, in some way, change the focus of the group. When you are supposed to listen intently to your children, spouse, or a colleague, you might suddenly feel the urge to eat something, check your phone for no reason, or remember something in your life that relates to what they're talking about, and you want to mention that. We must learn to recognize the attacks of the Flesh and how to die to them.

PRAYER
Resist Temptations of the Flesh

Dear Heavenly Father,

I come in the Name of the Lord Jesus Christ and ask You to show me the way that my flesh is keeping me from being the loving and righteous person that I can be. Open my eyes to how I am giving in to the temptations of the Flesh without even realizing it. I ask for Your power and wisdom to resist these selfish desires. Please make it clear to me the loving things that You want me to do instead of the fleshly things I so often do. Thank You for forgiving my sins and working with me to grow into the kind of person You want me to be. I am amazed that even though I will never be perfect in all of these things, You keep working with me and empowering me to get better and more pleasing to You.

In the Name of the Lord Jesus Christ,

Amen

Weapon #2: Die to the Flesh

The Scriptures tell us that everyone has a natural tendency toward selfishness, and we often promote it beyond normal levels. It is not wrong to be self-interested, but it is damaging to be self-focused, self-centered, or willing to harm others to get what we want. When we give in to these impulses to indulge our wants, desires, and pleasures, we are falling victim to the Flesh. The temptations of the Flesh originate from within us. But fortunately for us, God has fashioned another weapon to win against these selfish impulses that go beyond normal levels.

There are a number of passages in Scripture that talk of dying to fleshly indulgences when we feel their urges (see Romans 6; Galatians 5; Colossians 3). Scripture presents the idea of dying to the selfish urge; in moments of non-responsiveness, we are to cry out to God for what He wants us to do instead. Then we quickly do whatever God prompts us to do. In that way, you will have defeated the temptation to indulge your selfishness. Let me show you this first in Romans 6:

> Even so consider yourselves to be dead to sin, but alive to God in Christ Jesus. Therefore, do not let sin reign in your mortal body so that you obey its lusts, and do not go on presenting the members of your body to sin as instruments of unrighteousness; but present yourselves to God as those alive from the dead, and your members as instruments of righteousness to God. (Romans 6:11–13)

When we feel prompted to slander someone or express our anger or sensuality, we are to die to that urge and live to what God prompts us to do.

Galatians also gives us a rundown of various selfish temptations we will face in our lives:

> Now the deeds of the flesh are evident, which are: immorality, impurity, sensuality, idolatry, sorcery, enmities, strife, jealousy, outbursts of anger,

disputes, dissensions, factions, envying, drunkenness, carousing, and things like these, of which I forewarn you, just as I have forewarned you, that those who practice such things will not inherit the kingdom of God. (Galatians 5:19–21)

These are excessive expressions of our pleasures and desires. They harm others. One of the major spiritual enemies we all face is the excessive selfishness that lives within us. This depraved desire to have what we know will be bad for us or bad for others keeps us from being loving people. We must find a way to keep from giving in to these temptations, attacks, and oppressions by learning how to die to our flesh.

SPIRITUAL EXERCISE
Fighting Against the Flesh

God gives us a powerful two-step weapon to defeat fleshly temptations:

1. Die to the temptation;

2. Listen to God's promptings for what to do instead.

Whenever you feel tempted to give in to a selfish urge that you know you shouldn't give in to, you can learn to die to that prompting (i.e., become non-responsive to it). This would be like when you feel anger about something rise within you, but you don't let it out in words or actions. Or when you feel fear or worry about something, but you refuse to let it consume your mind, and you focus on other thoughts and ideas. Or when you want to give in to urges to drink, take drugs, overeat, or look at pornography, but you refuse to act on it, dying to its implementation, waiting for different instructions. After you have become non-responsive to the temptation (you can do this with practice and prayer), then pray that God will prompt you with something else to do instead of what the temptation wants you to do. God will direct you with something to do, say, or think about. If you focus on doing, saying, or thinking about that new thing, you will beat the temptation.

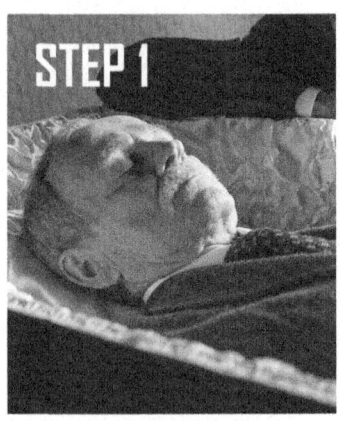

Weapons to Defeat the Flesh
A Powerful Two-Step Weapon to Defeat Fleshly Temptations
Step 1: Die to the temptation.
Step 2: Listen to God's prompting for what to do instead.

Usually, when this happens in my life, and I pray for God's direction, He puts a picture in my head of the dirty dishes, a vacuum cleaner, someone to call, or a good deed I could do. Now, in my opinion, it must be God putting these things in my mind because I would not think of these things naturally. When I quickly move to do what God is prompting, the power of the temptation goes away.

Try this two-step method to resist temptation the next time a fleshly temptation comes along.

Reflect on the past week. Which temptations have you encountered? Pride, Envy, Anger, Lust, Sloth, Gluttony, or Greed? Any from the list presented in Galatians 5:19–21? Which of these has been the most persistent?

Get ready for that temptation to come again; this time, you will die to your responsiveness to it, refusing to let your words, actions, or emotions express or engage with it. Then, during that death to the temptation, you will ask God what you need to do instead to beat the temptation. Then go and do what God suggested. This biblical method will work, and you can get better at using it.

First Corinthians 10:13 says that God has not left us alone; in fact, He is actively guiding us when we encounter temptations and provides a way of escape every time:

> No temptation has overtaken you but such as is common to man; and God is faithful, who will not allow you to be tempted beyond what you are able, but with the temptation will provide the way of escape also, so that you will be able to endure it. (1 Corinthians 10:13)

In many cases, we have been trained by our rationalistic culture not to pay attention to God's counter-prompting when we're in the middle of a temptation of the Flesh. But you will begin to win against temptation at a whole new level when you use these weapons together. It will also be proof that God is alive and active in your life.

Fleshly impulses are very immediate and can seem overwhelming. They want you to act on what they are prompting. If you are like me, when I was not very practiced at dying to anger, I would feel anger rise, and I would yell, punch, or let my anger out in some way before I had time to think. I had to learn how to slow the whole process down in order to use this biblical method. I put a card in my pocket to help me remember what to do in the heat of my anger.

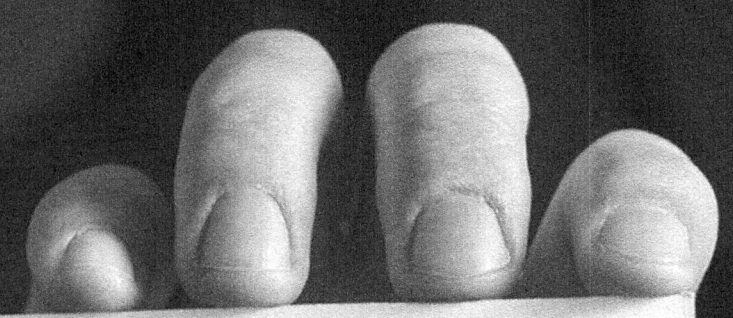

Stop,

Feel the anger,

But don't act,

Ask what God wants to do instead.[12]

I would pull this card out every time I felt the slightest anger rising in my body. I had to pull it out a lot at the beginning. This physical process of slowing down my anger was very effective.

Realize that the weapons to defeat each enemy are different. If you use the "Do Not Love" strategy against the Flesh, you will lose those battles. Worldly temptations are much subtler and longer-lasting and require Do Not Love strategies. Fleshly temptations are immediate, and you need an immediate way to combat their power. What works is dying to these urges (becoming non-responsive) immediately and then becoming quickly responsive to the righteous impulses of God. When a fleshly impulse hits you, you don't have much time to resist it like you would if you were tempted to start loving some part of the world. Slow the temptation down by becoming non-responsive to the pride, envy, anger, lust, sloth, gluttony, or greed that is trying to take over, and then immediately respond to God with what He is directing you to do.

PRAYER
Help Me to Hear Your Options

Dear Heavenly Father,

I come in the Name of the Lord Jesus Christ, asking You to help me recognize and slow down my response to temptation. I ask for Your wisdom and Your power to not respond to the selfish temptations to pride, envy, anger, lust, sloth, gluttony, or greed (you can pray about the specific temptations you face rather than the whole list). I want to do Your will and will need to listen to the promptings of Your Holy Spirit, so please make them clear. I will think, speak, act, emote, or intend in whatever new way You want me to move because I really want to beat this temptation.

I realize that I must, in this way, work out my salvation with fear and trembling (Philippians 2:12-14). Thank You for working with me as I grow in this ability to resist the temptations of the Flesh. I am grateful that You do not expect perfection on the first try. You just want growth. I also appreciate that You are full of grace and mercy. I will face many battles, some of which I will lose in various ways before I consistently win over the temptations I am facing now.

In the Name of the Lord Jesus Christ,

Amen

Understanding Enemy #3: The Devil

We have talked about two invisible enemies that try to make our lives a struggle. It is now time to talk about the third invisible Enemy, the Devil. He is not more powerful than the other Christian enemies, but he is a personal being and able to coordinate and follow up on the attacks of the World and the Flesh, so it may seem that he is behind every temptation and attack you face (Ephesians 6:12). The Devil and his demons are personal angelic sources of evil coming against those who want to live a righteous, loving life. They come at us in different ways than the World and the Flesh, so we need to understand how they will tempt and attack us. Let's spend some time looking at what Scripture says about this unique source of evil.

Satan is a fallen angel who was formerly known as Lucifer (Isaiah 14:12–14; Ezekiel 28:12–18). His demons are the angels (one third of all the angels) who joined him in rebellion against God's righteous rule (Revelation 12:3–4, 7–9). The Devil and his minions want to swamp you with emotions, stray thoughts, or evil opportunities. In this way, it is your own decisions that lead you in the wrong direction. It's important for you to realize that your own choices will be what doom you or bless you (Galatians 6:7).

The World, the Flesh, and the Devil can only present opportunities to act in destructive ways. You have to choose to act on their temptations and opportunities. The Devil wants to set up your choices, feelings, and thoughts so that you doom yourself to a life of uselessness, cynicism, or evil. The fiery arrows that the Devil fires at your soul are distracting emotions, disruptive thoughts, and/or evil choices (Ephesians 6:16). He does not show up in a red suit with a pitchfork and try to physically stab you. His weapons are spiritual, mental, emotional, and relational. They are meant to distract you, so you miss opportunities and destroy your potential, so you cannot live out your purpose. He oppresses you so you can barely function and keeps you from God's best path for you (John 10:10).

Spiritual Exercise to Understand the Devil's Attacks

The Bible is clear that the Devil has ways he typically uses against people to keep them from being righteous and loving people. These are the schemes of Satan. God tells us what these schemes are in the names that He has given to the Devil in the Bible.[13]

Take a look at this short list of Satan's various names according to Scripture and get a feel for the attacks he runs on us. Circle the ones he has used on you. Realize that he will keep using the same schemes against you that have worked in the past. Until you show that you can resist a temptation or an attack from him, he will keep using the same one.

The Devil (Revelation 12:10): an accuser, a slanderer, spreading lies and rumors against you, or using you to spread lies, gossip, and slander about others.

Satan (1 Peter 5:8): an opponent, an adversary, someone opposed to you, or you being the enemy to someone else who is trying to do some good thing.

The Tempter (Matthew 4:1–10): using a desire to distract you from truly loving or being righteous, or using you to be a temptation to someone else to distract or dissuade them from doing some righteous or loving action.

A Roaring Lion (1 Peter 5:8): using fear to keep you from doing something you know you should do, or using you as the roaring lion to incite fear in others so they will do the opposite of what they should do.

An Angel of Light (2 Corinthians 11:14; Galatians 1:8): using spiritual power or wisdom to lead you astray or keep you from doing the job of being righteous or loving in your normal life, or using you to be a source of false wisdom, power, or spiritual light to others.

The Dragon (Revelation 12:3,4,7,9,13,16): using anger against you or through you to manipulate the situation or keep you from being righteous or loving or being a source of anger or fear in other people's lives.

Beelzebub (Matthew 12:24–27): tempting you to be perverted and vile to get your way, or accepting this underworld way of thinking as normal, or using you to lure people into a vile lifestyle or a criminal existence. He wants to make a normal life seem too far away to even hope for after participating in this whole other underworld life.

The God of This World (2 Corinthians 4:4): using pride, ego, and arrogance to flatter you or others around you so that you are too important to do the normal, righteous, and loving actions you should do, or using you to puff up others or direct others through your importance or control to diminish or destroy parts of their lives.

PRAYER
Help Me to Protect Myself

Dear Heavenly Father,

I come in the Name of the Lord Jesus Christ and ask You to begin to show me the schemes that the Devil is using against me to keep me from being loving and righteous. I thank You that You see all these manipulations and attacks, and that You can give me eyes to see them and ways to protect myself against them. Show me how to resist these temptations and attacks. I ask that You give me wisdom and power to no longer fall victim to these ploys. I want to be a loving and righteous person. Show me how to do that, and the little choices I can make that will align my life with Your plans for me. Thank You for all that You are doing for me and in me. Thank You for Your forgiveness, which keeps covering me as I work out the salvation You have given me.

In the Name of the Lord Jesus Christ,

Amen

Weapon #3: Resist the Devil

God warns us that there will be times when the Devil and his demons will attack us directly without the use of intermediaries like the World and the Flesh. When a direct attack of the Devil and his demons comes upon us, it doesn't work to not love the World or die to the Flesh. Those tools will not work against this enemy. Instead, the weapon that works against the Devil is resistance! Notice what Scripture says in Ephesians 6:10–20 (emphasis mine):

Finally, be strong in the Lord and in the strength of His might. Put on the full armor of God, so that you will be able to **stand firm** against the schemes of the

Devil. For our struggle is not against flesh and blood, but against the rulers, against the powers, against the world forces of this darkness, against the spiritual forces of wickedness in the heavenly places. Therefore, take up the full armor of God, so that you will be able to resist in the evil day, and having done everything, to stand firm. **Stand firm** therefore, having girded your loins with truth, and having put on the breastplate of righteousness, and having shod your feet with the preparation of the gospel of peace; in addition to all, taking up the shield of faith with which you will be able to extinguish all the flaming arrows of the evil one. And take the helmet of salvation, and the sword of the Spirit, which is the word of God. With all prayer and petition pray at all times in the Spirit, and with this in view, be on the alert with all perseverance and petition for all the saints …

Four Key Steps to Win Against the Devil

In the extensive passage above on spiritual warfare, God outlines four steps for successfully battling the Devil. The first three steps I will cover in this chapter, but the fourth step is so full and so consequential that it needs its own chapter; in fact, it is its own weapon system, so it is really Weapon #4.

Step #1: Ask the Holy Spirit to fill you.

To win against the Devil, we need to be strong in the Lord and in the strength of His might (Ephesians 6:10).

Four Key Steps to Win Against the Devil

Step 1: Holy Spirit: I need the Holy Spirit's strength and power (Eph. 6:10). Ask for God's wisdom, power, and direction to live for God.

Step 2: Schemes: I need to understand the schemes of the Devil (Eph. 6:11). God told us what schemes the Devil will try to do: Tempter, Devil, Satan, Roaring Lion, Angel of Light, Dragon, Beezlebub, God of This World.

Step 3: Continue Love: I need to continue to love God, others, and myself righteously, even though it is a struggle (Eph. 6:13). God wants me to continue meeting needs, pursuing, and pleasing, despite the pressure to do something else. The Devil wants anything other than love.

Step 4: Armor of God: I need to put on the whole armor of God (Eph. 6:13-18). Ask for Truth, Righteousness, Peace, Salvation, Faith, Word of God, Prayer, and Alertness.

To get the Lord's strength and might, we need to ask the Holy Spirit to fill us with His wisdom and power, or we will not win. This is the Lord's fight you are in, and He knows what to do to win. There will be times when you do not have the strength to resist the Devil's attacks and temptations, but God does. Lean into what He is whispering to you in those moments when you want to give in to depression or sin or rage or immoral pleasure. Draw on His strength and might.

PRAYER
Fill Me with the Holy Spirit

Dear Heavenly Father,

I come in the Name of the Lord Jesus Christ, asking You to right now fill my mind, will, and emotions with Your Holy Spirit. I will listen and obey. Please make it clear what I am to do. I confess my sins to You. Show me the ways that I have been sinning against You and others and blocking Your work in my life. I plead with You to fill my soul and my body with Your Holy Spirit (Ephesians 5:18) so I can resist the Devil effectively as Jesus did during His temptation (Matthew 4).

In the Name of Jesus,

Amen

Step #2: Understand the scheme Satan is running on you.

To successfully battle the Devil, you must grasp which scheme he is using against you in this particular attack (Ephesians 6:11). Is it the "Tempter" scheme: excessive temptation? Is it the "Devil scheme": excessive gossip or slander? Is it the "Satan" scheme: excessive opposition? Is it the "Roaring Lion" scheme: excessive fear? Is it the "Dragon" scheme: excessive anger? Is it the "Angel of Light" scheme: excessive wisdom and power from the wrong source? Is it the "Beelzebub" scheme: excessive, immoral, corrupt, and harmful actions? Is it the "God of This World" scheme: excessive pride, arrogance, bigotry, or greed? How is he coming after you? Understanding which scheme the Devil is pushing on you allows you to prepare for those pressure points.

Scheme of Satan	What This Scheme Tries to Make You Do:
Tempter	Excessive temptation to go beyond a commandment or getting you to be the tempter for another person.
Devil	Excessive desire to gossip or slander, whether it comes at you or you do it about others.
Satan	Excessive opposition to something good and righteous, or you are the opposition to something good and righteous.

Scheme of Satan	What This Scheme Tries to Make You Do:
Roaring Lion	Excessive fear that paralyzes you, or you are the source of fear for others.
Dragon	Excessive anger aimed at you, or you are the excess anger aimed at others.
Angel of Light	Excessive spiritual power or wisdom being offered to you, or you are offering it to others outside of God's boundaries.
Beelzebub	Excessive vile, corrupt, degrading sins being offered to you, or you are offering them to others.
God of This World	Excessive pride, arrogance, or narcissism being offered to you, or you are offering it to others.

I would suggest that you make a copy of this table and put it on the bathroom mirror, the refrigerator, your phone, or in a card in your pocket or purse so you can quickly reference it.

PRAYER
What Scheme Is the Devil Running Against Me?

Dear Heavenly Father,

I come in the Name of the Lord Jesus Christ, asking You to give me a clear understanding of the schemes the Devil is running against me. Please give me discernment to resist with new effectiveness. How is the Devil trying to get me to give in to his schemes or participate in a scheme against another person? Please give me Your strength, resources, and new approaches to resist what the Devil is trying to push or lure me into. Thank You for helping me understand these schemes.

In the Name of the Lord Jesus Christ,

Amen

Step #3: Resist the Devil and keep loving.

The whole point of the Devil's attack is to stop you from being a righteous and loving person. To win this battle, you must continue loving God by practicing the spiritual exercises and loving those around you by meeting their needs, pursuing their souls, and pleasing them when you can. This is not the time to save your energy and take time for yourself. This is the time to ask God how to love Him and others more effectively.

"God, show me how and who to love in new ways that fit the time I am in." "Is there some new way that I can love You and the people in my life?" "Is this attack from the Devil trying to stop a particular kind of love that You want me to try in this season?" Ask God for His energy to expand your ability to love Him. Ask for His energy to increase your love for other people, especially those closest to you. Ask God for His energy and discernment to righteously love yourself. Thank Him for this test of your faith and plunge forward with His love.

PRAYER
Expand My Love

Dear Heavenly Father,

I come in the Name of the Lord Jesus Christ, asking You for wisdom and power to love more effectively. I ask You to show me new ways to love in this present season I am in. I ask You to show me the specific actions of love that the Devil is trying to stop by this attack, temptation, or oppression. I ask You for the energy to expand my love for You. Give me wisdom and power to increase my love for those closest to me and for any other people You want me to love more. I ask You to give me energy and discernment to love myself more righteously. Thank You for this test of my faith, so I can learn new levels of love.

In the Name of the Lord Jesus Christ,

Amen

Weapon #4: Put on the Armor of God

We learned how the Devil wants to stop you from becoming a loving person, so he will run predictable schemes against you. To win against these schemes, you will need the Holy Spirit's power and wisdom to effectively resist (Step #1). You also need to know which scheme the Devil is running against you (Step #2). And you need to know the ways to keep loving God and others (Step #3). Now we learn Step #4—how to strengthen our spiritual force field by putting on the full armor of God.

The Devil and his minions want to swamp you with emotions, stray thoughts, or evil opportunities so that your own decisions send you in the wrong direction. He may do his Tempter scheme, Devil scheme, Satan scheme, Roaring Lion scheme, Angel of Light scheme, Dragon scheme, or the God of This World scheme. But whatever scheme he tries to run against you, you have a God who wants you to win. Ephesians 6:10–20 outlines the necessary protective spiritual attributes that Scripture calls the armor of God. As a maturing believer, you must learn to resist by using the eight weapons God has provided. Let's review these magnificent weapons.

THE FULL ARMOR OF GOD

Truth

Righteousness

The Gospel of Peace

Salvation

Faith

The Word of God

Prayer

Alertness

WEAPON #4: PUT ON THE ARMOR OF GOD

As a pastor and teacher of spiritual warfare methods, I am often asked what the common denominator is in those who are repeatedly attacked by the Devil, especially in severe ways. As I said earlier, and what I believe is crucial to understand, is that there is some sin that has been committed and needs to be cleaned out through confession, repentance, and renunciation. We must depend on Christ's sacrifice to forgive and cleanse us, not our own works or efforts. But I would say that I also see a certain level of ignorance in most Christians these days about how to understand and utilize the armor of God.

I think we get caught up on the pieces of the centurion's uniform that Paul describes, and we get off track on what he was actually saying, so let me spell this out as simply as I can. Apart from those who are in a situation similar to Job's, there are people who are under constant severe attack from the Devil. They are missing one or more of the weapons Paul talks about in some way, namely: truth, righteousness, peace, salvation, faith, the Word of God, prayer, or alertness. To overcome the Devil's attacks, they need to incorporate these qualities into their lives in a way they haven't done in the past. Let's look at how to do this for each weapon.

TRUTH

If someone is being attacked or oppressed, it could be

because they have embraced some lie about themselves, God, the world, their spouse, their future, their worth, or their abilities. Therefore, they need to put on **truth**. They need to hold onto whatever truths are under attack in their mind, repeating how they know these things are true. Put on truth and strengthen yourself in the Lord Jesus. Allow the Holy Spirit to move you forward in the truth that God is directing you toward.

I can remember a woman who was plagued by her family-of-origin issues. She was thrown out of her house at fifteen and felt worthless and abandoned. She eventually became a Christian when she met and married a nice young man who began taking her to church. She didn't make progress in her depression and feelings of worthlessness until she began to hold on to the truth about the value she has in God's eyes. She is a child of God. She has been redeemed by grace. She has no condemnation on her because of what Jesus did for her. She is headed to heaven despite her sin and her family's assessment of her. Whenever she began to believe the voices of the past, her feelings of depression, worthlessness, and abandonment came rushing back.

RIGHTEOUSNESS

If someone is being attacked or oppressed by the Devil, it could be because they have a hole in their **righteous-**

ness. Either they are trying to earn their own way into heaven instead of trusting Christ completely for their entrance into God's family, or they are refusing to clean up some clear unrighteousness in their life. Perhaps they are resisting doing positive, righteousness (love) to the people in their lives. Put on the righteousness of Christ and begin doing practical, God-directed righteous actions. In this way, you are resisting the Devil.

I know of a young man who struggled deeply with anxiety and inadequacy. One day, he began to realize that he did not have to be adequate; Jesus had already been adequate in every way for him. Jesus had done all the work and had accepted this young man through His grace. When he realized these truths, he began to make progress because Christ had supplied all the righteousness that he needed. He did not have to be perfect; in fact, he knew he was not going to be righteous on his own. He was able to battle the Devil in his mind, who was accusing him of his need for perfection, with the righteousness of Christ for him.

PEACE

If someone is being attacked or oppressed by the Devil, it could be because they have a missing amount of **peace** in their life. They could be missing peace with God through Jesus Christ because they do not really embrace that they, as a sinner, are declared righteous through their faith in the work of Christ. It could be that they refuse to be at peace with someone with whom they are quarrelling. It could be that they do not want to let bitterness, a grudge, or resentment go over a past hurt. It could be that they are not willing to move past a past hurt and are hanging on to vengeance, missing the life they could have had if they let it go. Put on peace and forgive people so you can move forward with a positive impact.

I talk to people all the time who have an enduring bitterness because someone has deeply wronged them. One man was going through a family wound over an inheritance. He put on the peace of Christ and agreed to forgive his brother and to work with him to find what was just for all the family members. When he forgave and sought peace with his brother, God began to move. The family estate was peacefully settled, and the whole family profited. When he put on peace through forgiveness and wisdom, the attacks stopped, and there was peace in the family.

SALVATION

If someone is being attacked or oppressed by the Devil, it could be because they have not embraced the **salvation** of God in some way. It could be that they have not truly surrendered to Jesus Christ as Savior and Lord. It could be that they are unwilling to take the way of escape that God is offering in their present difficulty because it is hard, ego-deflating, or for some other reason. Put on the salvation that God has provided and move forward.

A young man came to see me who was plagued by demonic attacks. He had tried to commit suicide and was eventually committed to a mental institution because of his bizarre thoughts and actions. A friend of his asked that I talk to him and pray with him, so I took a group of us to visit with him. As we talked and prayed, it was clear that he was highly intelligent but was also under regular spiritual attack. We talked with some of the demons plaguing him. We tried to cast them out but were making little progress. We asked those in the group with gifts of discernment of spirits what the problem was, and they said, "unbelief." As we explored that in prayer and with the man himself, it was clear that he did not want to believe in Jesus Christ as his Savior and Lord. He just wanted the voices to stop plaguing him. We explained that without embracing Jesus Christ, there was no power over these voices. After over an hour of working with him, he did not want the gift of salvation; he just wanted the voices to stop. Finally, we just gave him the right to make his eternal choice. We told him how to receive Christ Jesus as Savior and Lord through the prayer of faith. We prayed for him and wished him well, and I have heard that he still has never accepted Christ and is still committed to the mental institution.

FAITH

If someone is being attacked or oppressed by the Devil, it could be because they are struggling with **faith** in some way. It could be that they are resisting or are ignorant of the doctrines of the Christian faith. It could be that God is asking them to trust Him for something that is not consistent with who they are or who their family is, and they are resisting. Put on faith and move forward.

I know a young lady who is a hero of the faith. Almost every day for many years, she had been plagued by worry, anxiety, and fear. She has learned how to hold up the shield of faith, trusting God to do the next right thing. She plows ahead as a wife, a mom, and an employee, even though at times she wants to just curl up into a ball and give up. But she trusts God to give her the strength to do the right things in her life. Just recently, God has given her a whole new level of energy to do the right things in her life, and her anxiety and fear are almost gone. She is a hero because she walks by faith and not by sight or by feelings (2 Corinthians 5:7).

WORD OF GOD

If someone is being attacked or oppressed by the Devil, it could be because they have a problem with believing, understanding, or knowing the **Word of God**. It could be that they do not know enough of the Word of God for God to speak to them out of it. It could be that they have not examined the reliability and accuracy of the Bible enough. It could be that God wants to speak to them through a section of Scripture they have not studied or explored, and it is not making sense. Put on the Word of God and take new spiritual ground in your life.

I was teaching a class at Jessup University on the Old Testament and showed students how to prayerfully read Proverbs and Psalms each day, allowing God to guide them and grant them wisdom. The very next class, a woman came to me very excited about how God had shown her a particular verse that completely answered a problem she was having. She had prayerfully asked about her number one problem in her life that day. Then she prayerfully started reading the Proverb for the day slowly. God just lifted a verse off the page and made her pay attention to it. She almost immediately realized that this verse was for her. She changed what she was doing based on the verse, and the problem was solved. She was so excited that God had directed her through the Word of God on how to deal with one of the real problems in her life. She had put on the sword of the Spirit and used it.

PRAYER

If someone is being attacked or oppressed by the Devil,

it could be because they are in some way deficient in **prayer**. They do not know enough of the different ways to pray to have a fully developed spiritual life. It could be that they are trying to be too spontaneous in their prayers or too rote. It could be that they do not know the scriptural and historical guides to a deep prayer life. Put on prayer and watch God support you.

The other day, our family was praying about a situation one of our children was facing. There didn't seem to be a solution. My daughter was getting discouraged because she needed an invitation from a university to start her Ph.D. She had been in the process for months. It was a critical time. I sensed that God wanted me to hunker down and pray very specifically for this issue, this blockage. I spent considerable time pleading with God to remove this blockage and get my daughter an invite to a Ph.D. program. The next evening at dinner, my daughter said that one of the university professors had invited her to apply so she could evaluate her doctoral research question and her application. It was a direct answer to prayer that happened the very next day after a period of considerable prayer. We rejoiced! She then received another invitation to apply to a different program at the same university, so she will also apply there. Put on prayer and ask God to remove obstacles, give power, show the right path, and do miracles that need to be done.

ALERTNESS

If someone is being attacked or oppressed by the Devil, it could be because they are not **alert** to how the Devil is scheming against them. It could be that they have grown complacent about some sin or vulnerability from their past. It could be that they will soon be facing an attack from the Enemy that is new to them, and they have not made themselves ready in some way. It may be that they are proud or arrogant in an area and, in that way, have let their guard down. This weapon calls us to be alert for the evil day so we can win.

I was working with a pastor years ago who, all of a sudden, saw his church explode with growth. People were coming to faith, and the atmosphere was dynamic in the church. The pastor was learning new skills and new ideas of leadership. God was moving and changing the nature of the whole town because of what was happening in this church. The pastor had never experienced this kind of revival fire before in any other church. It was incredible! Unfortunately, he began to think he was somehow causing it and let his guard down. All kinds of people were now being attracted to the Lord operating in him. One beautiful young woman started hanging on his every word. He was flattered and refused to keep proper boundaries when it came to private time with members of the opposite sex. Eventually, the Devil encouraged an affair with this woman. He lost his position at the church when the affair came out, and the church was significantly diminished through their sin.

This man lost everything because of his lack of alertness to the possibility of an affair, despite repeated warnings from his staff to set boundaries. He had a lovely wife and family. And because he was not particularly handsome himself, this issue had never been a problem before. He refused to see that this woman was sent as a tool by the Devil to destroy the work of God, not because she found him irresistible.

SPIRITUAL WARFARE EXERCISE:
Praying on the Eight Weapons of Armor

For this spiritual exercise, I want you to envision a force field around you, with each of the eight spiritual

weapons surrounding you. If one of these areas is weak, it can create a breach in the force field, leaving you vulnerable to attack.

If you sense you are in the middle of a demonic attack, pray through this list, asking God what you need to focus on to defeat the Devil. You obviously need them all, but there is often one or two that are the focus of your need, and why the Devil is getting through to you in his attack.

Pray, is it **truth**? Is it **righteousness**? Is it **peace**? Do you need a new level of **faith** and trust in God? Do you need a refocus on your **salvation** from your sins in Jesus? Do you need a specific verse or passage of **Scripture** that will guide you around, through, or over this pressure? Do you need to **pray** in very specific ways or about specific things? Do you need to become **alert** to vulnerability in your life or a particular kind of demonic attack you are not expecting?

Go through each piece of the armor and put on that piece in prayer until you are covered with truth, righteousness, peace, salvation, faith, the Word of God, prayer, and alertness. I have given you an exercise below to help you pray and listen to the Lord in greater detail.

Truth
First, ask God, "Lord, is it truth that I'm missing? If so, what is it?"

Pause and listen to what truth you need to lock onto; listen for the lie the Devil is peddling; listen to the Holy Spirit in your spirit and your soul about areas that you don't know enough information, enough wisdom, enough understanding of what is really going on.

Cry out to God for the truth you need to resist and win against this temptation, this attack, this onslaught. Bring the lie that is attacking down to size with the specific truth that diffuses the work of Satan.

Righteousness

Ask God, "Lord, is it righteousness?"

Pause and listen for the guidance of the Holy Spirit, whether you need to remind yourself that you are not worthy to go to heaven, or that you are only going because of what Jesus Christ did on the cross. You are unworthy, but in Christ, you have been forgiven and accepted as a child of God.

Listen for a specific righteous action that God wants you to take that will block the Devil's attack. Is it to confess a particular sin and repent from it? Is it to love and benefit someone in your life who needs it? What is the Spirit saying to you?

Peace

Ask, "Lord, is it the gospel of peace?"

Pause and listen for the whispers of the Holy Spirit

that you are at peace with God because of what Jesus did through His life, death, resurrection, and ascension. Is God asking you to forgive someone for how they hurt and wronged you? Is He asking you to leave all vengeance with Him to handle?

You cannot put on the gospel of peace if you are still at war with someone. Let God guide you to mourn your losses and bless those who curse you. Let the Lord empower you to focus beyond the offense, hurt, and trauma. Let the peace of God settle on you, focusing on the positive, the loving, the joyful, and the kind things in your life.

Salvation

"Lord, is it salvation?"

Pause and let the Lord whisper in your soul that you have been delivered from the domain of darkness. You do not need to listen to or obey the impulses and actions of the past. Let God show you the way of escape He has designed in your present situation. Listen when God brings someone to mind who could help you understand a solution or deliverance in this situation.

Faith

Ask, "God, is it faith?"

Pause and see if God tells you where He is asking you to trust Him specifically. He will get specific, so do not be vague in your trust.

Let God know that you are listening and tell Him you will trust Him about the core issue(s) in your present difficulty.

Let the Holy Spirit by faith show you the future when you are past this problem and are declaring God's glory through how you overcame this issue with God's guidance and power.

Word of God

"Is it the Word of God?"

Pause. Do you need a new dose of salvation, a very practical way of escape, or a solution you don't know about yet? Let the Holy Spirit get you into the Scriptures and strengthen you through His words of Life.

Set aside time every day to study and meditate on new sections of the Word of God. Read through familiar sections like Proverbs and Psalms to let God direct you to the wisdom you need for that day.

Prayer

Ask, "Lord, is it prayer?"

Pause. Do you need to explore more forms of prayer than you currently know? Do you need to become more skilled in prayers of confession, listening to the Holy Spirit, biblical meditation, Bible study, request-based prayers, service-based prayers, adoration, praise, gratefulness prayers, communion prayers, witnessing-based prayers, surrender-based prayer, and generosity-based prayers?[14]

If you are going to converse with God, you will need to be familiar with these forms of talking to Him and listening to Him.

Alertness

Ask God, "Is it alertness?"

Pause. Do you need to be alert to areas where the Devil is setting you up to be defeated? Is there some area where you have fallen in the past that you are not as vigilant in? Is there some new kind of scheme that the Devil seems to be running against you? Are you becoming too confident and proud, thinking you can't be tempted or sin in some area?

In the Name of the Lord Jesus Christ,

Amen

SPIRITUAL WARFARE EXERCISE:
Resist by Using the Armor of God

When you are swamped by overwhelming emotions, bombarded by evil choices, or assaulted by stray thoughts that seem off or evil, resist them by pushing back against them with one of the pieces of spiritual armor.

First, start by comparing these thoughts, emotions, and opportunities with what you know to be **true**. What is true about you, about Christ, about your past, about God, about righteousness? Don't give in to the desire; choose the right path. Ask God to show you the truth you need to embrace and keep in mind.

Next, run these thoughts, emotions, and opportunities up against the weapon of **righteousness**. Would Jesus do this? Would a righteous person I know do this? Would a righteous person tell me to do this? Resist the temptation to be unrighteous. Ask God to show you the righteousness you need to adopt and act out in your life. Is it accepting the righteousness of Christ? In what way do you need to act righteously? What unrighteousness do you specifically need to avoid in your present situation?

Then move to the gospel of peace. Run these ideas, feelings, and opportunities up against **peace**. Would doing whatever it is make peace? Does doing this thing suggest that I am not completely forgiven in Christ? How does doing, feeling, or thinking this thing make me more connected to Christ or more peaceful as a person? Don't allow the Enemy to get you to choose a bad direction. Ask God to show you how to stop any strife with another person. Ask God to show you how to forgive anyone who wronged you. Ask God to direct you on how to live in harmony with someone in your life. Thank God for the peace He is giving you so you can move forward in love and not bitterness.

Next, align these thoughts, emotions, and opportunities with **salvation**. Does whatever it is move me more toward Christlikeness? How does doing this thing make me full of the grace of God? Can I imagine myself doing anything like this in heaven? Don't give in; resist. Ask God to show you what His salvation in your life wants to do rather than these ideas, feelings, or opportunities. Ask God for His way of escape from this pressure or demonic temptation. Let the Lord know that you will take God's way of escape if He makes it clear.

The Devil hates it when we use **faith** to test his attacks, temptations, and opportunities. Does whatever it is make me trust God more? How does thinking, feeling, or doing what this attack wants me to do build my trust in Christ? Don't give in to trusting yourself and your own wisdom. Ask God to increase your faith to trust Him for more blessings. Ask God to deepen your understanding of faith and how the doctrines of Scripture answer the temptations of the Devil. Thank God for the examples in Scripture of people who have trusted God in the face of all kinds of obstacles and temptations.

Let God prompt you with the **Word of God**. As you think about these ideas, emotions, and opportunities, what verses come to mind? Are these ideas, emotions, and opportunities in agreement with the Bible or in conflict with it? What verses suggest that I should think, feel, or do these things? Ask God to give you a verse or verses to help you discern and defeat the lies of the Devil, just like Jesus was given in His temptation. Ask God to show you which character from the Bible will offer insight into your situation. Ask God to show you more wisdom and understanding in the Proverbs and the Psalms for the day.

Put on the armor of **prayer**. As you think about the current situation that is causing so much difficulty, talk with God about all of it. Tell Him about your feelings. Share with Him the benefits and the negatives that you are contemplating. Don't just ask one question, but ask dozens of questions in your discussion with God. Ask God if you should be thinking, feeling, or doing these things.

The Devil's ideas, emotions, and opportunities should be seen as warnings and as weak points in our defenses. **Be alert** to a warning light in the areas that you have given in to him in the past or to ways he has tripped up other people because they have fallen asleep about some kind of temptation or attack. If the Devil is working this hard to get you distracted, what is he trying to distract you from? The goal of the Devil is not to get you to sin—the goal of the Devil is to get you to not be righteous in some way. What righteous good thing won't happen if you think, feel, or do what the Devil wants? Don't give in to his desire to get you to choose a bad direction.

PRAYER
Putting on the Armor of God

Dear Heavenly Father,

I come in the Name of the Lord Jesus Christ, asking You to show me the truth that I need to instill in my mind. I ask You, Lord Jesus, to show me the righteousness that I need to put in my life. Is it the righteousness of Christ? Is there some way that I need to act righteously? Is there some unrighteousness I specifically need to avoid in my present situation? Lord, I'm putting on Your righteousness that is completely enough to satisfy God's standard. Thank You, Lord, that I do not need to be perfect; You have been perfect for me. Let me rest in Your sacrifice for me. I ask You, Lord, to show me how to stop any strife with another person. Show me how to forgive _____ who wronged me. Please, Lord, direct me how to live in harmony with _____ who is in my life. Thank You, Lord, for the power to overcome the difficulties in my life.

I right now put on Your salvation accomplished for me. There is no condemnation on me; it landed on You, Lord, thank You. Show me, O Lord, what Your salvation in my life wants to do rather than these temptations, feelings, or false opportunities. I ask you, Lord, for Your way of escape from this pressure I am facing. Lord, I will take God's way of escape, just make it clear. I ask you, God, to increase my faith to trust You for more blessings and clearer ways to love God, others, and myself righteously. Please, Lord, deepen my understanding of the Christian faith and how the doctrines of Scripture answer the temptations of the Devil. Thank You, Lord, for the examples in Scripture of people who have trusted God in the face of all kinds of obstacles and temptations. I ask you, Lord, to give me a verse or verses to help me discern and defeat the lies of the Devil just like Jesus was given in His temptation (Matthew 4). Show me what character from the Bible will offer me insight in my situation (Psalm 19:7). I ask You to highlight a verse in the Proverbs or in the Psalms so I will have more wisdom and understanding from You.

Lord, I am being troubled by these ideas about _____, these emotions of _____, these opportunities to _____. I don't know if they are from you or from the World, the Flesh, or the Devil. I need to talk with You about all of my thoughts, and I want to understand what You think and feel about all of these things. Lord, here is what I am feeling about these issues. I want to talk with You about the benefits I see and the consequences that could take place. I need You to help me see more than I can see in this.

Lord, I have so many questions and emotions about this situation. Thank You for listening. Please let me know if I should be thinking, feeling, or doing these things. Show me, O Lord, what these ideas, emotions, and opportunities I am vulnerable to. I ask You to help me build up my defenses against the areas that I have not even considered in the past. Give me guidance on who I need to talk to so I will be more knowledgeable and prepared for these kinds of attacks, temptations, and oppression. I thank You, Lord Jesus, for giving me this spiritually protective armor and for showing me how to put them on. I need all of this—put it on me and show me how to use it effectively.

In the Name of the Lord Jesus Christ,

Amen

CONCLUSION

I hope you have been doing the spiritual exercises in this book and are growing into new levels of maturity. It is through doing and practicing the spiritual exercises that we actually grow. It is not enough to just know new information, we must become skilled in these ideas.

Remember, there is only one goal for spiritual warfare: to love God with all of your heart, soul, mind, and strength and your neighbor as yourself. You are winning as you become a better lover. If your fight with the Devil does not release you into becoming more loving, then something is wrong. Always ask, *What is the loving action that God wants me to do and the enemies He wants to keep me from?* The battle you are facing may be just a distraction to keep you from loving a crucial person in your life. Ask for God's power and wisdom to see what the real battle is about. The spiritual battle for many businesspeople is realizing that the people in their family matter more than making more profit and having more customers. For some people who take care of their family, they're fighting a war that can only be won when they keep loving, even when they receive little cooperation or gratitude.

Every Christian's faith must grow and push through to new levels of spirituality. The Scripture talks about at least three stages of faith: little children, young men, and fathers. One of the crucial elements in growing in our faith is becoming strong in the Word of God so we can take on the Devil. God wants us to become more impactful, and knowing the Scriptures is key. It is very encouraging that people are beginning to want to do battle in spiritual warfare. This tells me that God is trying to raise up the next generation of mature Christians who are learning to take on the Devil and gain the ability to love more effectively and powerfully.

> And this I pray, that your love may abound still more and more in real knowledge and all discernment, so that you may approve the things that are excellent, in order to be sincere and blameless until the day of Christ; having been filled with the fruit of righteousness which comes through Jesus Christ, to the glory and praise of God. (Philippians 1:9–11)

We also saw that there are three levels of spiritual warfare: mild, moderate, and severe. The levels of the spiritual battles are directly linked to the types of sin in a person's life. If a person has lots of Sins of Omission, they will face mild spiritual temptation, attack, and oppression. If a person has been committing Trespass Sins, or Sins of Commission, and has not confessed these to the Lord, there will be a significant increase in the level of temptation, attack, and oppression in their life. If a person is practicing sin and living beyond the boundaries of the Ten Commandments in some area of their life (Wickedness), then they are facing severe temptation, attack, and oppression. Wherever we find sin, we need to agree with God that it is wrong, repent, and head in a different direction than the sin, and, finally, renounce any power or place we gave to Satan by our involvement in that sin.

Our three enemies who consistently want to keep us from becoming mature, righteous, and loving are the World, the Flesh, and the Devil. Our struggle with the World is one that conforms to values, behaviors, and lifestyles that are not biblical. The World is trying to deceive us by getting us to love what is temporary and false. It wants us to love its answers to life's questions, even though they don't work long term. We are to win against this creeping pressure to adapt to the wrong answers by not loving the ideas, answers, values, and rewards of the World. We are to love the Kingdom of God, the relationships God gives us, and the blessings and rewards He bestows.

The Flesh is a selfish, distorted image of ourselves that is always with us. It wants to assert itself in every decision and situation. It wants us to take out our selfish desires on our souls and our bodies. If we let this selfish and sinful image of ourselves become the consistent version of ourselves, then we will miss God's best for us. We need to wage war on this distortion of our true selves by dying to the impulses of the Flesh and living in God's direction and wisdom. In this way, the righteous, loving, and godly person we really are meant to be will emerge.

The Devil wants to destroy us as effective and wise lovers of what really matters: God, others, and our righteous selves. He plans ways to keep us from being loving, mature Christians by running schemes against us. If he can get us caught up in his temptation schemes, slander and gossip schemes, opposition schemes, fear schemes, false spiritual power and wisdom schemes, anger schemes, perverse schemes, or ego-pumping schemes, he keeps us from loving and making a godly impact. How many people have been shipwrecked because of these schemes? God tells us that we need to be filled with the Holy Spirit. When the Holy Spirit is dominant in our lives, we become aware of the Devil's schemes, commit to loving God, others, and ourselves righteously, and ready ourselves for battle by putting on the full armor of God.

Armed with these truths from Scripture, you can begin to win against the three main enemies of the Christian. You can become a wise lover of God, of others, and yourself. There will always be more ways you can grow in the Christian life, so keep growing and keep loving until you see Him who has been from the beginning face to face.

I'm praying for you as you fight back to win the life God wants for you.

NOTES

[1] These two commands to love God and to love our neighbors in Matthew 22:37–39 are what we should do. Any time we fail to love God or love others when we should is a Sin of Omission.

[2] In the Lord's prayer, Jesus asks that we forgive others of their trespasses just as we want God and others to forgive us our trespasses (Matthew 6:9–12). These trespasses over the lines of the Ten Commandments are Sins of Commission.

[3] Peter tells Simon Magus that he is in the grip of wickedness and needs to repent (Acts 8:20–24).

[4] I detail all of these in the book *Becoming a Godly Husband*.

[5] I detail all of these in the book *God's Radical Plan for Wives,* a collaboration with my wife, Dana, and Jennifer Edwards, on how a wife should approach these commands.

[6] I recommend investigating *Christian Financial Concepts* with Larry Burkett and *Financial Peace University* with Dave Ramsey.

[7] Gil Stieglitz., *Becoming Courageous: Facing Your Past and Building Your Future* (PTLB Publishing, 2014).

⁸ Gil Stieglitz., *Spiritual Disciplines of a C.H.R.I.S.T.I.A.N.* (PTLB Publishing, 2011).

⁹ Anonymous, *The Martyrdom of Polycarp*, Ch. X, in *The Apostolic Fathers* with an English Translation, ed. and trans. Kirsopp Lake (London: William Heinemann, 1912).

¹⁰ Gil Stieglitz, *Spiritual Disciplines of a C.H.R.I.S.T.I.A.N.* (PTLB Publishing, 2011), 19–20.

¹¹ I go into much more detail on the positive counterparts in my books *Deep Happiness* and *Becoming Courageous: Facing Your Past and Building Your Future*.

¹² Gil Stieglitz, *The Anger Reset: 27 Days to a Calmer You* (PTLB Publishing, 2025).

¹³ Gil Stieglitz, *The Schemes of Satan* (PTLB Publishing, 2015). These are the basic schemes of Satan, and this book will allow you to explore the Scriptures and ideas more thoroughly.

¹⁴ Here are five resources that I have authored on prayer and three other prayer resources: *Spiritual Disciplines of a C.H.R.I.S.T.I.A.N.*; *Touching the Face of God; Going Deeper in Prayer*; *Getting God to Talk Back*; *They Laughed When I Wrote Another Book on Prayer*. Other great works on prayer are *E.M. Bounds on Prayer*, *Intercessory Prayer* by Dutch Sheets, and *Rees Howells Intercessor* by Grub and Percy.

ABOUT THE AUTHOR

Dr. Gil Stieglitz is a prolific author, engaging speaker, and insightful pastor who has written over thirty books on marriage, parenting, soul development, and spiritual warfare. Other books on spiritual warfare include *The Anger Reset: 27 Days to a Calmer You* (Book One in his Spiritual Warfare Series), *The Schemes of Satan, Satan and the Origin of Evil, Why There Has to Be a Hell, Breaking Satanic Bondage,* and *Weapons of Righteousness.*

Gil speaks to thousands of people each year about the wonders of God's wisdom and principles. He currently serves as a discipleship pastor at Bayside Church, a dynamic multi-site church near Sacramento, CA. He founded Principles to Live By (PTLB), a nonprofit organization that helps people connect to God's principles in everyday life. He and his wife, Dana, reside in Northern California and have three adult daughters. For more information about his books and speaking, visit www.ptlb.com.

OTHER PTLB RESOURCES

Spiritual Warfare and Personal Transformation

The Anger Reset by **Dr. Gil Stieglitz**

Breaking Spiritual Bondage by **Dr. Gil Stieglitz**

Spiritual Disciplines of a C.H.R.I.S.T.I.A.N. by Gil Stieglitz

Becoming Courageous by Gil Stieglitz

The Keys to Grapeness by Gil Stieglitz

Deep Happiness by Gil Stieglitz

Secrets of God's Armor by Gil Stieglitz

The Schemes of Satan by Gil Stieglitz

Satan and the Origin of Evil by Gil Stieglitz

Why There Has to Be a Hell by Gil Stieglitz

The Gift of Seeing Angels and Demons by **Dr. Susan Merritt**

Weapons of Righteousness by Gil Stieglitz

Uniquely You Workbook by Jenny T. Williamson

For additional resources and to learn about the mission and purpose of Principles to Live By, visit PTLB.com. Books are available at Amazon.com, Barnes&Noble.com, and Target.com.

Made in the USA
Coppell, TX
13 January 2026

68263678R00095